The Bush Still Burns

The Autobiography of William T. Lowery Sr.

*Reaching Out to the Lesbian, Gay,
Bisexual, and Transgender Community*

DEDICATION

To my son,

Michael P. Lowery,

And to the other seven children of a blended family,

And to two of my grandsons, who encouraged me to write my autobiography.

Thanks!

ON THE PSEUDONYMS USED IN THIS WORK

In some cases, I was unable to obtain permission to use the names of people who are part of my story. Where that has been the case, I have placed a carat (^) alongside the pseudonym I selected for their representation.

"Now Moses was tending the flock of Jethro, his father-in-law, the priest of Median. And he led the flock to the back of the desert, and came to Horeb, the mountain of God. And the Angel of the Lord appeared to him in a flame of fire from the midst of a bush. So he looked, and behold, the bush was burning with fire, but the bush was not consumed."

Exodus 3:1-2 (NASB)

CONTENTS

PROLOGUE

"The bush was not consumed." Moses was born and raised on the Nile.
He returned to his people and killed an Egyptian at forty years of age. He
fled the Pharaoh. He trekked across the wilderness of Shur to the desert
of Midian. He tended the sheep of Jethro, his father-in-law, for forty
years. He led the sheep to the backside of the desert to the foot of Horeb,
the mount of God. He saw a bush that was burning; but the bush was not
consumed. God spoke, "Take your sandals off your feet, for the place
you stand on is Holy ground. Come, go set my people free." He took his
wife Zipporah and two sons and re-trekked the wilderness of Sinai to
Pharaoh's court. "Let my people go." After ten signs, the Pharaoh agreed
to let "God's people go." Moses and the Israelites fled. The waters
divided. Pharaoh's army perished. Forty years they traversed the
wildernesses of Sinai. Finally, they rounded the southern tip of the Dead
Sea and skirted the barren lands of Edom, Moab and Ammon. Israel's
army defeated Sihon, king of the Amorites and Og, king of Bashan.
Moses instructed God's people once again; he encouraged Joshua to be
strong and of good courage. They settled on the plain of Jordan opposite
Jericho. Moses climbed Mount Nebo to view the 'Promised Land'. God
buried him there. Later, Moses and Elijah would visit with Jesus on the
Mount of Transfiguration – God is the God of the living not of the dead.
Moses had taken off his sandals to serve God with bare feet, and to
worship God on Holy Ground at Horeb the Mount of God. On bare feet
of service he served God, and he worshipped Him on Holy Ground in
Heaven!

APPRECIATION AND GRATITUDE

It is with Thanksgiving that I thank everyone for their part as I have written my autobiography, The Bush Still Burns. I give thanks to the Rev. Dr. Jeffrey P. Johnson, Superintendent of the Mid-America Conference and the executive Director of the Men's Ministry International (MMI). His timely messages brought me to my knees at Lighthouse Christian Camp on July 1st 2013. His wise counsel to me personally was priceless, and his suggestion helped me to choose a format for this book which has been a blessing to write. I want to thank the Rev. Ronald Sawade and the Rev. Todd Daningburg, pastors who encouraged me to write and to step "out" into a new community. I want to thank two congregations for their support. When I could hardly believe in myself, they believed. Thanks, Valley Chapel and Ransomville Free Methodist churches. I have been sick for the last two and a half years. Finally, I needed family care. I could not continue to do for me. I want to thank William Jr. and his family for their loving and timely care of a sick, old man. I have asked him to provide the foreword for my book, and I especially asked that he permit me to place in the appendix his great sermon, "Murder on the Nile." I thank my son and his family, because this book has become a family affair. My grandson, Joshua Lowery, and his lovely wife, Alyssa, have jumped aboard to help with the overall format and editing, respectively. He asked me to write it and he introduced me to his then bride-to-be by asking me to share my testimony with her over brunch. I want to thank my entire family who, without exception, has encouraged me in writing. I have felt their prayers. I thank the many, many people who have prayed and encouraged me through small groups, jail ministry, and more, and those that have asked for copies to read when I have finished my autobiography. God bless each of you. And, I thank Mr. Compute, my trusty computer, for helping me to correct typing and grammatical mistakes caused by dyslexic fingers. Last, but not least, I want to worship my Lord with this verse from His word. **"Thou art worthy, O Lord, to receive glory and honor and power: for thou hast created all things, and for thy pleasure they are and were created."** (KJV) I worship with 'Thanksgiving' my great Triune God, with an **Amen,** Jesus!

PREFACE

I am on a journey, and only God knows where I am going until I arrive there. I have aimed for Heaven, but God has me on detours. Remember that I am writing about life experiences; I am not writing about being homophobic or about gay bashing. I want to take you with me on a journey that has spanned eight decades of homosexual struggles and issues. Six of those decades have been as a Christian whose struggles have included four wives and eight children in blended family relationships. I have walked a life of integrity during those decades.

I have elected to write my autobiography in letter format. I begin each chapter with a letter to Myke, breaking my life down into life Periods in a devotional format that will explain these relevant life periods. My biography will deal with extended family and the church. My aim is to reach out to the lesbian, gay, bisexual and transgendered community (LGBT) in all of its facets and give that community a glimpse of the hope that we have in Jesus Christ that will be easy for them to grasp.

Equally, my aim is to show the Christian world and the Church how we can reach out to the LGBT community in love through the life of a man of faith. I have lived in the closet until recently; I do not know how to do this; however, I am "Out of the Closet and about my Master's business"! Also, I do not believe that the church has any idea how to bridge the gap between the gay non-believer and Jesus Christ. Jesus said, **"Go and make disciples of all nations."** (Matthew 28:19 NLT) They are a part of all nations.

I have a formidable journey ahead of me to reach people I care about with the Gospel, and I am not sure how to go about the task or to arrive at my intended destination. May I challenge you to journey with me? My goal at this time is not to gay-bash, but to offer to those that read my autobiography the chance to make a decision.

The question is simple, "What decision is God asking you to make personally that will bring you closer to Him and enable you to celebrate a life of Eternity with Him?" That is a simple question, but it will not be an easy one to answer! The answer will always be by faith.

Section One

An Autobiography

PART ONE: MY EARLY CHILDHOOD

I remember Samuel. His Mother Hannah trained him until he was weaned. And, she presented him to the Lord. I think of Jesus. Mary kept all these things in her heart and she pondered them. One day, He would say to His parents, **"Why did you seek Me? Did you not know I must be about My Father's business?"** (Luke 2:51 NKJV) I can see Samson. There was a handful. And finally, I remember a first step to get my books at exactly seven months. I can remember saying 'No' and at the same time his continuing to do what he was doing as I was helping him to understand what I wanted him to do. I remember a daughter who gets mad every time I again remind her, "You can't run away." It was a challenge. I grin. Now, I remember and thank God for parents who trained and were patient with me; and sometimes for good reason were not so patient. **"Honor thy Father and thy Mother."** I do and I remember with humility!

A Letter to Myke

Dear Myke,

I am writing to you because we are alike in many ways. I want you to know who I am. The first thirteen years of life are important. They permit people to get to know each other. We did not have that privilege. I am proud that you became my son by adoption on January 27, 1983. I will be breaking my life story up into periods of time with natural breaking points for you to get to know me better and to learn what makes me tick. There was oral tradition that formed my life.

I was born on a Monday, October 25, 1926, during a snow storm in the middle of Jefferson County, just off the road from Port Barnett to Knox Dale, Pennsylvania, about one mile from Meade Chapel Episcopal Methodist Church. The church sits in a bend of the road surrounded by farming country. There are a couple of farm houses in sight, and the Meade Chapel Cemetery lies immediately to the south of the Church. I was born north of the Church on a narrow country road that led to the Carr Farm. I'll have to draw you a map sometime. Our nearest neighbors were about a half mile away from the farm. Later, those neighbors would see that I got to school and first grade.

The Carr farm was situated on some rolling hills. The farm belonged to my paternal grandmother and her husband, Franklin Carr; because of the depression we had nowhere else to live. We had lived in my early years in Munderf, PA; Olean, NY; and Claremont, NH by the time I was about four. My mother and father told me bits and pieces of events that happened during that time period. She told me that she had a job in a hotel in Olean as a cleaning lady making beds. My father told me he worked in a coal mine near Munderf, PA, and I can just remember that he had travelled to Akron, OH and worked in the Firestone Tire Factory. Also, he told me that he rode the rails through the West during the dust storms, looking for work. I can remember Franklin Delano Roosevelt's "Fireside" chats.

It comes time to tell you how I was developing and the things I remember during those pre-school years. I am going to do this by attaching some devotionals I have written that will help explain who I am and how I got here. They will include first memories. They will explain that I have never liked to be alone and what I did on the farm, and they should give you a glimpse of parts of me that I have never before conveyed to anyone.

Yours in love,

Dad

Learning to Read

"In the beginning was the Word, and the Word was with God, and the Word was God." (St. John 1:1 KJV)

Sometime in the Spring of 1933, I was learning to read. In the Old Farm House, there was a kitchen, a living room, and three bedrooms for at least twelve people and sometimes more. On one spring afternoon I was in the kitchen where my mother was engaged in her favorite pastime: crocheting.

I had been given a little red paperback Gospel of St. John, but I have no idea who gave it to me. I was about six and a half years old. Since the school was two and a quarter miles over dirt roads and farm land, I was sent to school the following Fall. The weather was rough in the hills around Meade Chapel, Pennsylvania.

I do not know how I learned some of the words. But, that wintry sunny afternoon, I would make my way over to Mom's chair where she was engaged in her favorite past time, and I would ask "What's this say?" with my finger pointed at a particular word. I wanted to know what the letters were, how to pronounce the word, and what it meant. I have no idea how many times I made my way to that chair. I know I did not get all the way through the first chapter. I believe the clincher came on the word "believe" or it may have been "receive." About this time, mother exclaimed, "Billy, I'll be so glad when you go to school and learn to read," only after she had dropped several stitches. In retrospect, I have two reactions. One is that I laugh at what my mother said to me. The other is that I realize that I was accomplishing the desire she had just expressed.

My Father in Heaven, I thank you for your Son, Jesus Christ - The Word of God. I thank you for my learning to read and to express in words my love for You. To this day, I am still learning to read and to use new words because the "Word was God," and with the aid of my mother, I was taught to read. Amen!

Oral History

My personal edited definition of "oral history" is the systematic collection of living peoples' testimonies about their own experiences, passed from one generation to another. I want to convey to you what I picked up about my own early years.

I have read many stories about people who lived through the Great Depression. My life has spanned the presidencies of fifteen United States Presidents, beginning with the 30th president, Calvin Coolidge, until the present. Coolidge was the President when I was born, and was followed by the 31st President, Herbert Clark Hoover. Hoover was elected in 1928, within months of the stock market crash of October 29, 1929 which occurred on what is now known as "Black Tuesday." I do not remember the details, but my mother had nothing good to say about his presidency.

I can remember President Franklin Delano Roosevelt and one of his fireside chats in the summer of 1932. My uncles, Archie and Melvin, had gotten a Crystal Radio Kit and assembled it on the kitchen table in the old farmhouse. It was powered by a battery from the farm tractor. I cannot remember what he said, but I can remember his voice. I would later be proud to serve my country in the United States Navy during his term of office. FDR was elected in November of 1932, and was the first to achieve four terms as President.

I can remember things that happened to me during the Great Depression. I experienced them. Our family was poor, but I did not realize it. We didn't eat eggs. Instead, we took them to town to buy coffee, oleo, and absolute necessities. The only time you got an egg was when the hen broke it and the egg could not be sold. I know. One afternoon, I was hungry and Grandmother Carr went to the hen house to see if the hens had laid any eggs. Sure enough, there were two broken ones. I have often wondered who really broke the eggs, the hen or Grandma. They tasted good that afternoon. I can remember chickens that meandered through the kitchen and left behind a deposit, because we had no screens on the doors.

I can remember. We had no phone and no radios except the one mentioned previously. It did not work after that one occasion to my knowledge. We had no electric lights. There were kerosene lamps or lanterns in those days, or you got up with the chickens and went to sleep with them. It saved money.

I can remember one supper that included potatoes and green peas, thickened with flour. You ate what was put on your plate. Another meal I remember was with Pastor John Shafer. He visited us just before supper time. I do not remember what was served, but I do know this: after supper he read scripture and knelt beside the table on our not-so-clean floor. It was in the middle of the week, and we cleaned on Saturday. That incident did not discourage me from desiring to be a pastor when I grew up. If anything, it fired my determination. I wished that I had been more of a story-teller for my children as they were growing up, but I was often told, "Little boys need to be seen, not heard."

Father, I thank you for fond memories of growing up in hard times. They bring tears of joy to my eyes. I pray Father that those who read this will take this page out of my book and be able to tell their stories about what life was like when they grew up to their families. Amen!

First Memories

I ask you to read Psalm 139 before you continue to read this devotional. In verse four, we read, "For I am fearfully and wonderfully made; Marvelous are Your works, and that my soul knows very well."

This will probably be the hardest devotional I will have to write. It has to do with my earliest memories. The first was on the farm work road that went west as you came to the road leading to the farm. The road went past the wagon shed and the tractor shed, on west between the farmhouse, chicken pen, and yard, past the watering trough used for the horses and cattle, on westward to the pig barn, and on out into the corn field. My first memory was of playing with my sister in the middle of the road. The sand was nice and clean, and it gathered there after it rained. It made a good place to build sand castles, a childish construction site with sticks and stones. On this day, I had a "Bull Durham" sack, two stones, and a stick. I was in the process of using them to make my sister, two years younger than I, into a boy. I wanted a boy to play with. A "Bull Durham" cloth sack was about the size of a current day cigarette pack. The sack contained tobacco and had papers attached to the back so that you could roll your own cigarettes. I have no idea of the price, but I would guess that it probably cost about 25 cents. Needless to say, I did not accomplish the task. My mother caught me in the act. Years afterward, during family get-togethers, she would tell the story much to my personal embarrassment. My sister never remembered the incident.

My next memory occurred almost simultaneously with the one above, and it is of going with my father to feed the horses and animals in the barn. My job was to feed the chickens outside the granary by scattering grain for them to eat. The chickens were free to range for the rest of their needs. The men on the farm would hay the horses and cattle and take them to the watering trough, come back to the barn, put their harness on, and feed them grain near the plum trees that was near the sand pile. After which, we went to the farm house and ate breakfast, and after breakfast, the teamsters would go out to the plum trees and finish getting the horses ready for plowing or whatever the task was for the day. This memory is still vivid in my mind today.

Fanny, our light brown beagle, was the rabbit dog. She was housed next to the smokehouse which was just across the yard from the big side porch. I can remember feeding, playing, sitting, and talking with her many times. We had three other coonhounds who the men fed. My friend was a white dog with black specks all over him. Their pens were on the south side of the Cave house and it was separated from the farmhouse by about fifty feet. This next is both an oral and real memory. I can remember once, when left to myself, I stripped down and went to the old white coon dog's house. I wanted to share with that old coon dog an hour-long afternoon nap. There was no straw that day, but I shared a nap until mother came looking for me. I can still remember her scolding me. Not only did I detest being alone, but I had trouble sleeping by myself. I would get up, often undress myself, and go sleep walking. I did this until about third grade when one day Dad told me that he would douse me with ice water if I ever did it again. I remember that those incidents were retold again and again when family and friends were together. I still do not like to be alone. Simply stated, I want to be me, but not alone.

Today, I can pray with sincerity of heart the last two verses of Psalm 139:23-24; and 14A (NKJV).

"Search me, O God, and know my heart; Try me, and know my anxieties; and see if there is any wicked way in me, And lead me in the way everlasting. – I will praise You, for I am fearfully and wonderfully made." *Amen!*

The Call of God

"For the gifts and calling of God are without repentance." (Romans 11:29) KJV

"Marvel not that I said unto thee, Ye must be born again." (John 3:7)

I can remember being in church one time before I attended school. I recall sitting in the front row of the Church swinging my feet, looking out the window at the gravestone of my great-uncle David Carr, and watching Pastor John Shafer preparing to preach and the soloist for the day practicing the song she was to sing. I made this statement to myself: "When I grow up, I am going to be a preacher like Pastor Shafer." That was about 82 years ago. My mother had admonished me to behave myself. I am sure that as I swung my feet she was not too sure I was going to stay out of trouble.

I would like to say that I never wavered from that day to this, but that is not the case. I was in fifth grade when I went to the altar for the first time and gave my heart to Christ. After more downs than ups, it was not until I was twenty-six that, with the help of God, my life as a Christian really began to come together.

My affirmation on this occasion is that **"God's gifts and God's call are under full warranty -- never canceled, never rescinded."** *Romans 11:29 (The Message)*

Play and Work

"And we know that all things work together for good to those who love God, to those who are called according to His purpose." (Romans 8:28 NKJV)

It's often said, "All work and no play makes Jack a dull boy!" and I am sure that the reverse is true as well. I was a precocious boy, and as it turned out I was not dull by any means. One chore from which I was exempt was the mowing of the grass-- the animals and chickens that ranged took care of that task. I was, however, expected to help feed the chickens, to feed Fanny the dog, to help in the barn, to get water from the spring, to learn to milk Betsy the cow, and to help weed the vegetable garden. This work did away with the need for a baby sitter. There was nearly always an adult nearby to supervise.

I liked weeding the vegetable garden because my Grandma Carr helped make it fun. She told me how to do it and trusted me. The job was never too little, nor was it ever too large. The time it took to weed the onions was just right. She told you not to step on the lettuce, or it would not grow. Mainly, it was just fun to be with Grandma Carr. I still like to weed the garden, though it is a little hard on the back now. It did not seem to bother my back during the pre-school years. Grandma had one cow that was hers. She milked Betsy, and once in a while my Father would be entrusted with the task. It was fun when she felt I was old enough to learn to milk the gentle cow by hand. There was no milk parlors way back then. In my teen years, I would use the skill I had learned to milk goats.

Now, it is time to consider the other side of the phrase: 'play.' The prophet Zechariah prophesied concerning the restoration of Jerusalem, **"The streets of the city shall be full of boys and girls playing in the streets."** (Zechariah 8:2 NKJV) As I remember, there were no streets on the farm, but there were stone and dirt roads for wagons and the old Model T Ford to travel on. We did not have bicycles, so that was not an option. This begs the question, "What were your toys like?

One Christmas I ended up with a red metal dump truck, about 10 inches from one end to the other. Its saving features were that you could fill it with sand and dump it and that it had one "D" flashlight battery that powered the headlights. I took it everywhere, and I soon learned that if I left the lights on, the batteries would go dead. My sister got the delight of her life: a Raggedy Ann doll. A tinseled Christmas tree without lights, a little candy that was a special treat and a toy to enjoy made Christmas one special occasion. On another Christmas, my sister and I each received sleds. It was fun to slide down the hill from the blacksmith shop into the yard, and if you were brave and conditions were just right, you could go further up the hill to the orchard and really get a ride. We were not poor; we were living, working and playing with what God provided for us, in His divine wisdom.

PART TWO: COUNTRY EDUCATED

1 Timothy 4:11-14 New King James Version (NKJV)

[11] These things command and teach. [12] Let no one despise your youth, but be an example to the believers in word, in conduct, in love, in spirit, in faith, in purity. [13] Till I come, give attention to reading, to exhortation, to doctrine. [14] Do not neglect the gift that is in you, which was given to you by prophecy with the laying on of the hands of the eldership.

Father, I thank you for the country education that has been a blessing to me throughout the years. I have used that education to bless others in ministry as I have served your Church. Thanks. Amen!

A Letter to Myke

Dear Myke,

I want you to go through the elementary years of school with me. I was country educated. I went to one-room school houses for three years, with a single room for each of my third and fourth grades, and for three years to a two-room school house for fifth, sixth, and eighth grades, but not for seventh grade. The schools were not too far from each other. The seventh grade school was a one-room school about fifteen miles from the others, all in Jefferson County, Pennsylvania.

I began school on September 5th 1933. You may picture the circumstances. It was a one-room school with about 30 students covering eight grades. Pleasant Hill was about 2 ½ miles from the Carr farm where I lived. I was a little pipsqueak, very slight and not too tall. My first teacher was Ted Alcorn. I did not pass nor fail; because of snow days that I missed, I was put on probation. We enjoyed outside plumbing, and near the end of the year, about 20 minutes before dismissal, Mr. Ted would not allow me to go to the outhouse. I walked home with streaks going down my leg. It was embarrassing for me then, and it still does as I think back.

The distance was long, and because of that my Dad asked two girls to take me under their wings. Their names were Aldine and Geraldine, and they lived about ¼ of a mile away from our home. Somehow, they were related to my father by marriage. They were twins in the eighth grade. Geraldine was the one I was entrusted to for the most part. She was the quieter and more caring of the two.

The next year I went to Lucas School. Lucas School was much closer, about 3/4 mile from the farm. You need to remember that this was during the mid-part of the Great Depression. The district had just reopened the school, and Bill Alcorn, the younger brother of Ted, was my teacher for my second year of school. My father had attended the Lucas School when he was a lad. I have his certificate from when he graduated from the eighth grade. By the way, I passed both first and second grades that year. Mr. Bill was a great teacher. I can still remember him.

Things changed that year. Your grandfather was able to get a job drilling gas wells, so we could get a home of our own. After school was dismissed around the end of April, Mom and Dad decided to look for a house. They asked Mom's mother and father if she, my sister, and I could stay at their house while she looked for a house in Brookville, Pennsylvania. They said yes. I lasted one week. My mother found a home on the east side of the borough. The street was unpaved, but we had a yard of our own to play in, trees to climb, and plenty of ways to get into trouble. Longview Elementary School was at the end of the street. Each grade had its own room and teacher. My third grade teacher's name was Mrs. Davis, and my fourth grade teacher was Mrs. Tanney. She was a tall, robust woman. She gave the impression to her students of being like their own mothers.

My two grandmothers died during that summer following the fourth grade. Grandma King died from complications from gall stones, and Grandma Carr died after having a vaginal tumor removed. The differences between the two were in stark contrast. I loved them both, but I have often wondered how they could be so different in personality. Grandma King was a very strict Christian, but she was a very cantankerous person. There was no give or take in her. Grandma Carr was a Christian, I believe, who seldom went to Church. However, her main characteristic was that she was loving and kind. They were opposites. After their deaths, my parents were asked to come live with Grandpa King, since he was all alone. It is from him and Grandma King that I get my love for gardening.

We lived in Pine Creek Township. The house was up a lane, about a mile from the school. It was a two-room school house. Mrs. Pearsall was the principal and taught grades five through eight. I do not remember who the first grade through fourth grade teacher was. For my seventh grade, I went to a one room school house in Sigel, Pennsylvania. The teacher's name was Miss Annabelle Stack.^

A quotation seems appropriate here, "Elementary my Dear Myke". I would like to remind you that Sherlock Holmes, the famed fictional detective, would invariably say, "Elementary my dear Watson," as I remember, when solving a case. Thus, I close with this. The facts concerning the above will still be in a devotional style. This devotional style helps me tell my story in an easy manner; and at the same time very effectively. Heretofore, I have not described my family. This section will tell you how I grew up and answer questions about who I am and how I got there.

With love from

Dad

Seventh Grade

Myke, I could title this "Bears in the Woods," but this one year sticks out not because it was so great but because it had many tidbits of experiences in it. I was 13 when my dad got a job near Cook's Forest State Park cutting timber, since drilling for gas was shutting down for a while. Two young friends of Dad's were a part of the move, and they got jobs working with him as well. Clyde and John (not their given names) were about 21 years old. We moved about 15 miles from Grandpa King's house at Pine Creek to a house about halfway between Sigel and Clarington on route 36 North.

The first thing that happened was, as we moved in to the house, the base of the cast iron kitchen stove got broken. They solved the problem by getting bricks and setting it on them, and it was that way for the year that we lived near Cook's Forest. The next thing that caught my interest was that Dad's two friends smoked cigarettes. There was a large apple tree in the front yard which leaned at an angle. With the tree hiding us from the house, I had my first cigarette. I do not know where Dad was supposed to be, but suddenly he caught me. It was amazing to me, but from that time on I was permitted to smoke, and my Father supplied the cigarettes. I smoked until I was 26, and the volume increase from about a pack a week to three and four packs a day. I have never done things halfway.

I do not remember too much about my seventh grade education at the one-room schoolhouse about a half mile from our house. I do remember the teacher, Annabelle Stack^, who was just starting her first year of teaching. She was about five foot four inches tall, and she was relatively plump. The thing that was amazing was that she wore mini-skirts before women were wearing mini-skirts. One thing that happened was that after all of the parents were invited to the Christmas program she was not hired back the next year. I know this: the students did not suffer academically. At least, I know that I did not suffer. I was nearly always at the top of my class. The thing I did not enjoy was being quizzed verbally. I made sure that when that happened, I did nothing to draw attention to myself. If I was in a classroom situation to this day, I would make sure that I would not be noticed.

Bears were of interest in the area. About a half mile behind the house was a stand of pine trees. I remember walking in the woods and seeing bear spoor. When we went for a walk in the woods there always had to be someone with us, in case a bear was lurking around. I can remember one incident. Donald, a seventh grade friend, was visiting, and we got permission to go over to his house, which was about a country mile beyond the school house, to go fishing. I do not remember catching anything that day. We were walking along chatting away on the dirt road, and suddenly we heard a noise. Our chattering had aroused a mother bear out of a brush pile along with her two cubs. We wasted no time getting as far away from her as we could. I am thankful that the cubs were not as easily awakened as the mother bear apparently was. Donald and I made our way down the road safely. I thank the Lord for sleepy cubs.

This was the year when logging left its mark on me. I watched the three men sharpen their axes until they could cut a hair by laying it on their blades. I watched them in the evenings, sharpening their peaveys. I watched them learn how to sharpen the crosscut saws. There is just a certain way to do it. There were no electric saws or gas driven saws way back then. Two men each got on one end of the cross cut and back and forth it went until you heard "Timber." When you heard them holler, you made sure you were out of the path of the tree. My foster brother Clyde ^ had his axe down at his side, and as I heard "Timber," I stepped back and into his axe blade. I have a three inch scar on my left calf to this day. I was a picture of a little lumberjack then. My job when I was out in the woods was to pile brush out of the way. My pant legs were tucked into my boots. How Clyde's axe cut me without cutting through my pants or boots remains a mystery.

At home I had different tasks. I was needed to pile wood in the springhouse to keep the wood dry. Another one of my jobs was to bring the wood from the springhouse into the kitchen and the living room stove. You always needed a supply of kindling wood on hand in case the fires went out. I learned to split the fire wood. This summer at our

Christian Camp we needed a supply of kindling wood to get the fire going for a delicious meal and s'mores afterward. I still had the skill to meet the need at 86 years of age.

Today, I can praise the Lord for all the memories that are precious to me. And, I can join the Psalmist in the following: **"Let the field be joyful, and all that is in it. Then all the trees of the woods will rejoice before the LORD."** *(Psalm 92:12 NKJV) My heart rejoices before the Lord for all the precious memories of my life. Amen!*

The Flip-Side

"But we know that the law is good if one uses it lawfully." I Timothy 1:8 (NKJV)

"Even something good like the law can be used improperly. Its purpose is to teach us about right and wrong and to curb sinners." (The Wesley Bible)

I have said to myself many times, "I just want to be me." More properly, there were the times when I actually screamed those words in my heart. My dilemma has been that I am not who people think I am. Until I was 26, I lived two distinct lives. On the one hand I am the person that you have seen and known. However, there is a "flip-side" to this particular metaphor. There is the side that you have not seen or known, and on the other hand ever since I can remember, the side that I have known and experienced -- homosexuality.

I have never liked that word. The first time I heard that word used in connection to myself was in the last week of eighth grade on April 22nd and 23rd of 1941. On two occasions during that week, other students used that word in referring to me. On the 23rd at recess time, someone hissed the word at me as we went to recess. I did not like the way the word was expressed and I lingered behind to look up the word in the big School House Dictionary in the corner of the room. The definition was then, and still reads in my Random House Webster College Dictionary, "Sexual attraction to members of one's own sex or having sex with another person of the same sex."[1] I did not like the thought. I was embarrassed. Now, as I muse, I remember that there were at least three people that could have spilled the beans. Luckily, for me, I moved about eighty miles away for my freshman year of high school.

---

[1] Random House Webster's College Dictionary. (2000). New York, NY: Random House.

"No temptation has overtaken you except such is common to man; but God is faithful, who will not allow you to be tempted above what you are able, but with the temptation will also make a way of escape, that you may be able to bear it." *I Corinthians 10:13. (NKJV) Amen!*

Upper Level

"Study to show thyself approved unto God, a workman that needs not to be ashamed, rightly dividing the word of truth. (2 Timothy 2:15 KJV)

"Upper Level" refers to the fact that the Pine Creek Elementary School was a two story structure. The lower floor (one room) was for grades one through four, and the upper floor (one room) was for grades five through eight. I do not remember the lower teacher's name. However, I will never forget Mrs. Pearsall. That is all we ever called her. She is probably one of the main reasons for who I am today. She nearly always started her class off with a Psalm and prayer. I can recall many of those passages even today, and I can remember her praying. She was a great Christian.

She was tall and raw-boned, but she was very much a lady. She was as equally adept at opening the class every day as she was at teaching you how to diagram a sentence or to write Peterson style cursive writing. I can still write it. However, she had one flaw of which I am aware. I do not know the reason, but she had attachments to her glasses to keep her eyelids open. They would not stay open of themselves. As the day wore along, her eyelids would slip out from under the attachment and she could not see. I had the utmost respect for this teacher that helped form my life.

Our classes ran from September to the last of April. The farmers needed their seventh and eighth grade lads and gals to help plant crops for the year. We had four month summers then. Mrs. Pearsall, on the other hand, lived and likewise worked on the farm. She helped her husband and others to make hay, combine wheat, oats, buckwheat, etc. She purposely did this so that during the school year, when the seventh and eighth grade kids got out of hand, she would be able to take corrective action. She let us know she was up to the task.

In the following paragraphs, I want to tell you about myself and activities that will give you insight into my life as an 'upper level' student.

First, I was slight of build with not too much fat on my bones. The word was soon got out that I was a sissy. I have never liked to get hurt, nor did I ever want to hurt anyone else. If I was being picked on unmercifully, my oldest sister, who was in the fourth grade, would bang anyone over the head with her lunch bucket. I can hear our dad telling her to bang them over the head, and that he would get her a new bucket. And, she did and he did. She was bigger than I was.

Recess at 10:00 AM, lunch, and recess at 2:00 PM were always interesting occasions. During these times we would always get busy choosing sides for softball games. Two guys would choose who would play on their team. They would throw a bat up, catch it, and the winner would begin to pick their team members. I have never been good at games and gymnastics at any time in my life, and that fact soon became apparent. I was always the last guy picked after all of the girls had been picked. It did not help my self-esteem. A noteworthy fact is that all of my children were and are good at sports. They had great mothers.

My middle name is Theophilus. Back then, I did not appreciate it so much. You can get all kinds of twists out of it. Remember, I told you previously about Peterson's Writing Class? I received a commendation for my excellent writing skills. And in the center of my name was a lone 'T'. Norma^, a big sixth grade girl teased me to find out what it stood for, but I would not tell her. She kept teasing, saying, "Oh, I know what it is! It's Tillie – Tillie the Toiler." It was a name of a little girl in a comic strip when I was in fifth grade. The clincher was, by the time I was getting out of eighth grade, even my parents on occasion would call me, and you know it, "Tillie the Toiler."

I was by no means friendless. My best friend was Butch ^. I liked him and he liked me. He was everything I was not. He was a man, even in fifth grade. Everyone respected him, and when he was around I had nothing to fear. We were friends and not in any way that was wrong. I can remember one day sitting on the bank and eating lunch before beginning the soft ball game. He was not around. Another friend, Bud got onto me verbally. He ended up by calling my sister a whore. I did not like it, so I challenged him. At the edge of the school property was a gas regulator building. We went out of sight of the school and everyone gathered around to see Bud, who was bigger than me, beat me up. It turned out that I got him around the neck and was choking him to death, and would have done so if it had not been that Butch came by and separated us and thus prevented a tragedy. I would have not let go. Anger knows no bounds, and no holds are barred.

Mutual masturbation and gay activity came into play, but off of school property. There were three boys that would invite me over to play after school. It became a given routine. We played all the games that kids would play in those days, and then there was activity that was not exactly play. There was one occasion in the eighth grade that will let you know that I was learning to feel my oats in other ways.

On one occasion, in my final year at Pine Creek during the afternoon recess, I did the wrong thing. I had noticed this one girl who would on occasion go down into the woods with some of the bigger boys in the glass. I became brave and simply asked her for the privilege. She refused, and told Mrs. Pearsall of the event. When I came into the classroom, Mrs. Pearsall showed this not so big boy that she could handle him in no uncertain terms. The school, at that point, did not know what I did that was wrong, but I sure did! I am equally sure that it was not too long before the word leaked out.

And, yes, I can say, "Thanks for the lessons – the good and bad – that have made me the man that I am today, in spite of myself." Father, I thank you for the opportunities to **"Show myself approved unto my God, a workman not being ashamed but rightly living for your glory!"** *(2Timothy 2:15 NJKV) Amen.*

My Father

"Even if my Father and mother abandon me, the Lord will hold me close." (Psalm 27:10 NLT) "Honor your Father and mother." This is the first commandment with a promise. (Ephesians 6:2 NLT)

I continue writing and realizing that you cannot leave your parents, siblings, or family out of it. My parents were a real part of my life. I would like to honor my father by giving you a portrait of him. I remember my father from tales that he told. His name was Theophilus Wilson Lowry (Lowry is not misspelled). Everyone called him "Theo." He was born May 31, 1901.

He told of "riding the rails" out west in the 1920's looking for work. He told of the dust storms that were a part of that time. He told of working out in a gym in preparation to be a prize fighter. He told of working for Firestone Tires in Akron, Ohio and dating the owner's daughter. Each of the tales was slightly different and embellished each time he told them, but you knew that there was a lot of truth in them.

May I tell you about one occasion in the summer of 1936? We had just moved onto a street near the Longview Elementary School in Brookville, Pennsylvania. My Grandmother Carr was visiting us that Sunday afternoon. She was my father's mother and had remarried after my Grandfather William Cluth Lowry passed away in 1906. It was a beautiful sunny day. Suddenly, a big black limousine drove up the street going very slow. It turned around and came back down the street, and dad recognized the woman he had dated in Akron, Ohio. He did not keep his mouth closed and suddenly we were in the midst of a verbal battle between my parents.

It was on this occasion that my dad and I had a hassle that I can remember to this day. After the limousine drove away and things had cooled down a little, I went inside the home and asked my mother if I could go up to a nearby woods and play. She said, "Yes." As I left the yard, dad asked where I was going and I told him. He said, "No." I went back inside and asked my mother, and again the answer was "Yes." When I left the yard the second time, Dad's answer was again a resounding "No." My angry reply was, "Nuts to you." We must remember that dad was a driller and worked away from home. Most of the time, my mother was the one I could go to when I needed permission to do something. However, from about 2:30 -5:00 PM my dad had me say "Nuts to you" for the rest of the afternoon. To this day, if I become exasperated and say "Nuts" it is like a slap in the face. The memory brings me up short in my tracks, even if I am by myself.

Dad was a big man. He was six feet and two inches tall and weighed about 260 pounds. . He was broad shouldered and muscular, slim at the hips, with immense hands, and no fat on him. In 1941-42, at the beginning of World War II, he still drilled for oil in the oil fields of Bradford, Pennsylvania. The young men that would normally be tool dressers had gone to war. My dad taught me to dress tools on a standard rig when I was about sixteen. There were many times that he had taken me to work as I was growing up. I knew what needed to be done. I had learned by watching; now, I was learning by doing. One thing that sticks out of in mind was dressing a bit. The six-, eight-, or ten-inch bits had to be dressed and kept the right size or the hole would be too narrow to accept the next bit that was the correct size. I would heat the bit in the forge and use the chain falls to get it onto the anvil. You dressed the bit with 16 pound sledge hammers; the hammer handles were about three feet long. Please remember, at that time in my life I was about one hundred twenty pounds. When I pounded the bit with my sledge, I shook. My corner of the bit would not go where it needed to be. My Dad would graciously take his sledge with one hand on the end of the handle and reach across and out my corner would go. He was helping me. However, I can still feel how angry and frustrated I was because I could not do my job.

There were two things that he would not let me do. I could not grease the old steam engine, and I could not grease the walking beam on an eighty-four foot high standard rig. He felt it was too dangerous for me to do, but it still had to be done each shift. While he was doing my job, he asked me to do his job. I would get up on the driller's stool, let down the screw, and keep drilling away. I was proud. If I was able to step onto the deck of a standard rig today, I could still tell when to let the screw down and keep drilling. It was not all frustration.

My father was the type of man that a young teenage girl of about fifteen would see working on the road doing construction and say, "When I grow up, I am going to marry him." He was about twenty at the time. And, she married him at 17 when he was twenty-two, on September 4, 1923.

Father in Heaven, I give you thanks that I can remember the good and the bad about my parents and still honor my earthly father. Amen!

My Mother

My mother was Elma Cecelia King. She was born July 30, 1906, and was five years younger than my father. She was five feet and two inches tall. When my Father and mother married on September 4, 1923, she tipped the scale at a hundred pounds. They were a sharp contrast to each other. Father was a robust man and mother was a small dainty woman with pretty features.

My dad's father passed away in 1905 from pneumonia. Though he was left for a few years without a father figure, he was a man's man. Early in life, he learned to help his mother take in washings with his little red wagon as she supported herself and four children. My grandmother often told with pride how he would help her.

Mother's daintiness did not last long. I first remember her as a woman of about 180 pounds. She was not a strong woman, either physically or emotionally. She was plagued with eczema almost all of her life, and she had problems with digestion. I am sure that today she would be diagnosed with acid reflux and would have been given the normal prescription of Nexium, the purple pill, or a good anti-acid. She had this condition from about the time she was 30. Dr. McKinley told my Dad in about 1940 that he needed to get goats and give her goat milk or she would die. She passed away near her 73rd birthday and had no problems eating. In 1936, she had a nervous breakdown, and for a few years my sister and I helped Mom get through her problems.

I can remember that in third and fourth grade there were many occasions when I would get up and get our breakfast. I would fire up the old wood kitchen stove and make oatmeal or fry eggs for our breakfast. After breakfast, we would take care of the pets and go to school while mother slept. The breakdown left her with emotional problems that she and the family dealt with for years. When she was in her mid- 50s there would be times when she would search for my father. He worked near our home. When she saw him she would start running as fast as she could. As she ran to him she would be crying as if her heart would break.

There were great times in their lives as well as in ours as we were growing up. Mother and Dad celebrated their 25th anniversary in 1948 by going to Toronto, Canada. It was undoubtedly the highlight of their life together. I can never remember going on vacation as a family. However, I do remember going for walks on Sunday afternoons. We would pick flowers, trailing arbutus, from which mother made a tea for her health. It seemed to work. We would also pick boneset for Dad. In the winter, during the cold season, he would make a tea of it, and he never seemed to have the flu or a real dinger of a cold.

They taught us how to pick horseradish to put on our meat. My mouth waters as I think of it. A good roast or steak makes me drool. In the spring, there were always leeks. The smell never allowed me to get them into my mouth. These were the things that we did that brought joy to our lives and taught us to love one another in spite of the economy in which we grew up.

Mom always had her crocheting to keep her busy. I have no idea how many tablecloths, doilies, and other items that she would make just for fun and then give away. She and Aunt Edith, a friend, vied with each other in crocheting. Mother was a great seamstress. The old sewing machine was kept busy patching our pants. In my younger years she made everything I wore from the skin out. Dad was not exempt from getting new pants and shirts, etc. She was able to make dresses. During the depression years, you could not always buy cloth because you did not have the money. However, chicken feed came in sacks with pretty designs on them. They did not make too shabby of a dress.

Mother was not a pushover. I recall that she got me a fountain pen when I was in eighth grade so I could write decently at home. I was told not to take it to school, but one day I slipped it into my pocket. Somehow, she discovered what I had done. When I got home she confronted me with the fact. She did something that was unusual for her. She got the three legged razor strap that was used for extreme punishment. It was extreme. Another thing that happened that day was that when Dad came home he confronted me about what had happened. He laughed and told me that

Mom had done what he would have done. I was not to get corrected all over again that evening.

Father, I thank you for parents that loved me through the difficult years of growing up during the Depression. I did not realize I was a poor kid, but I did know that I was loved. Amen!

How Old Are You?

"The length of your days is seventy years - or eighty, if we have the strength..." (Psalm 90:10A)

Is age all in the way that you encounter it, or is it in all the way that you look at it? The Fall of 1934 gave me my first reaction to the question of age. I was in the second grade in Lucas School, in Jefferson County Pennsylvania.

It was customary for people in our community, during the Depression, to get a ride with the mailman on the morning mail run to Brookville to go shopping, and to return with him on his second trip in the afternoon. Mother was accustomed to doing this when the need arose. The mailbox was about a mile from the Carr Homestead where we lived. She would walk out in the morning and return with her purchases and mail in the afternoon.

On this day, she arrived at the Lucas School just as we were getting out for the day around 4:00 P.M. As we were walking home, up past the Ole Humphrey Hay and Straw barn, I asked her a question. "Mother, how old are you?" I can still see and hear her. She was wearing a white summer dress with red buttons down the front with a red belt buckle. She replied, "I am twenty-eight." I am sure that I did not voice my thoughts at that moment, but I thought to myself, "I hope I never get that old." I was a mere eight years old.

Now, as I sit, think, and write, I realize that 87 years have slipped by the board. I smile to myself and think, "Twenty-eight would not be all that bad right about now." Age, I find, is a matter of perspective. At times, I do not feel as old as the calendar tells me I am. But, I can feel blessed as I read Psalm 90 and know that God holds not only the memories, but the future in His all-wise hand.

As I reflect as a Christian, I am reminded of Psalm 92. **"The godly will flourish like palm trees ... Even in old age they will still bear fruit;**

they will remain vital and green." (Verses 12-14, NLT) Lord Jesus, it is with Thanksgiving that we remember the past and at the same time praise you for the years and wisdom you have so divinely extended to me. Amen!

Quirks of Life

I look back to August of 1933. I met Jack ^ only twice in my life. He was one year older that I was, and he had completed first grade. Like all boys of that age, we had to go to the bathroom in an old outhouse, and there was the necessary inspection of our private parts. I had never been circumcised, and had trouble with the end of my penis growing closed. As it started to bleed, I was scared and I did not share my dilemma with my family. It healed, thus far so good. The next year in August the same thing happened. Needless to say, I was introduced through no fault of my own to mutual masturbation. However, it would have its effect on me through the years of my life.

Memories are kind of scarce during my first and second grades. So, I want to skip to the summer of 1935. I had passed second grade and we were moving from the farm. It was interesting, to say the least, during that summer. Myke, please remember that in my letter to you, "I did not last too long at my Grandma King's that summer." It was one week to be exact. She had had her picture taken at the circus or fair. It was an old tin-type and it made her jaw look just like that of a Bull Dog. I was a precocious lad in those days, and I teased her about being my Bull Dog Grandmother. I pulled hers and my mother's apron strings on numerous occasions, and I teased my oldest sister who was two years younger than me without mercy. I was loud with never a dull moment for me. Needless to say, things were lively that week. I was just plain mischievous.

Dad was drilling that week. He came home on Saturday, and of course I was the topic of conversation. After dinner on Sunday, as he was getting to leave to go back to the rig at midnight, she let him know that I was no longer welcome. It was raining cats and dogs, as we used to say. My clothes appeared, and I was on my way out the door. I can remember standing on the porch. She handed out her big black umbrella to Dad with these words: "Here is the umbrella, and make sure you bring it back." I have never found out if the umbrella was ever returned. Too late now!

Dad and I made our way down over the hill and through the woods at the back of the house to the Pennsylvania railroad tracks for about 600 yards. We went east on the tracks for about a mile until we came to the place where we could get up the bank to the road that led from Brookville, to Knox Dale, Pennsylvania. It was about 500 yards up the bank. It was still raining, and there was another mile to Uncle Frank's. Dad had decided to ask his brother Frank and Aunt Huldah if I could stay there for a short while. That short while lasted all summer. I had a great time. This is the only time until my sister and I were grown that I can remember that we were ever separated. We were enemies at times, but it did not get between us. We were friends, and it always remained that way. We loved to fight, and we loved to get into trouble together. It was always my fault. I always protected my sister, except when she was protecting me.

Uncle Frank said I could stay there. I can picture the small room with a twin cot for me to sleep upon. Thus, I was alone. The below scripture will describe the rain as I experienced it that day, and the beautiful memory that it has left as I remember.

I am reminded of Noah and the flood. **"The waters prevailed and greatly increased ... and the water prevailed exceedingly on the earth**.*" It rained in the days of Noah. It rained that day! But, God gave a promise that he has fulfilled unto to this day. (Read, Genesis 7:17-18; 9:13-17. (NKJV); and I give thanks to God; because for every black cloud there is a rainbow.) Amen.*

Summer and Camping

We begin where the "Quirks of Life" ended, in a rain storm with only a big black umbrella as our protection from the elements. Uncle Frank was my father's younger brother. He was not as tall as Dad, but was very solid in his build. I would think about five foot nine. Aunt Huldah was his wife. She was a little shorter than he but about the same build. They did not have any children, so, for the summer, I was an only child.

I can remember from stopping there previously that she could certainly make delicious cookies. Yum! Ginger and molasses ones were my favorite with a glass of nice cold milk to wash them down. Everything that I can remember about that summer was fun. Aunt Huldah and I worked in the garden pulling weeds, picking radishes, and doing all of the easy things that can be a joy, especially to a small ten year old boy. I learned to pick strawberries and blackberries in season, and I am sure that I enjoyed those that did not make it into the berry pail. I got digs from briars. Those good things all happened while Uncle Frank drilled in the gas fields of western Pennsylvania.

The first night was a welcome surprise. I had a cot to sleep on in a room about eight by twelve feet. I never had that before. I shared a room with my parents and my sister. During the summer my Dad stopped by and checked up on me. I had no problems.

Two things happened that were new to me. One was that Uncle Frank had a motorcycle with a sidecar on it. Uncle Frank drove and Aunt Huldah and I were in the side car. That was fun. We went on a week's camping trip during the summer. They were taking a vacation. I remember taking all of the equipment to the campsite. I do not know where. We were by ourselves in the middle of nowhere. What boy would not want to go camping, especially with a motorcycle with a sidecar with a favorite Uncle and Aunt? After the setup, Uncle Frank took Aunt Huldah and me to the campsite with all of the food and extras that would be needed. We had a ten by twelve foot canvas tent. I was told that if it rained, not to touch the tent with anything or it would leak. It did rain one whole day. We were tent-bound that day, and I did not touch the canvas. I remember going fishing with Uncle Frank. I do not remember catching anything. I just know it was fun, and I enjoy the memory even as I write.

It was these things that I was not able to do with my Dad, Mom, and my sister that was worth the walk in the rain. I still wonder about the umbrella. Several years later they did have one child. Her name was Rose Mary ^. I can only remember seeing her once, about twenty years later. I have no idea how to even get in touch with her. I have worked on our family tree, and it has been to no avail. I'll just have to keep searching.

For whatever reason, summer and camping had to be a special time of memory and kept by itself. This reminds me that my two grandmothers have to logically become a part of my story at this point. They were as different as night and day.

My heavenly Father, I thank you for the memories of a summer that was special-- that began with one boy being mischievous, walking in the rain, and ending up with a wonderful experience – a summer that ended with a big rainbow. Amen!

My Grandfathers

Myke, I have heard it said, "We are a sum total of all that has ever happened to us." The easiest part of this section is my grandfathers. My paternal Grandfather, William Cluth Lowry, was born April 13, 1878 and died March 13, 1906. He was buried on St Patrick's Day. For whatever reason, that day has always been very special to me. He was 28years old. What I most remember about him was that he died from pneumonia. I received this information from my sister Edith. My father was only five at the time and was about twelve when his mother remarried. I do know that my father helped his mother to support the other siblings in the family by helping her take in washings with his little red wagon. He was proud that he was able to help his mother. Especially if he was reminiscing he would bring it up.

He did leave a legacy behind. I was told that eleven brothers and one sister had come over from Ireland. They owned Grey Abbey. It is Southeast of Belfast, Ireland, about 40 miles. I was told that we were Irish Catholic. However when Bill, Jr. and I visited Ireland in 2009, we found that the Lowery's came over from Scotland around the 1600's. We did see all that is left of the Lowry farm. We saw a piling that is still overlooking the Irish Sea between North Ireland and Scotland. The piling is about ten feet tall. Nearby is a Lowry Cemetery that supports what I know. Further, as I have researched our family tree, they probably came over somewhere around 1845-1852, during the potato famine, and they possibly landed on an Island in the St. Lawrence Seaway. To support this is the fact that I know that a Steven Lowry from Canada told me the same story in regards to his family as we happened to meet about 1962 in Franklinville, New York. The thing that my grandfather bequeathed to me was his love for detail. He kept a work diary. I have his diary and will pass it onto my family. The information may not be useful, but it is information that tells me who I am. Do you know what? I have the same knack for detail. I want everything to balance down to the last penny. I can praise the Lord for a grandfather and a father who passed down to me honesty in all dealings with mankind.

My maternal grandfather was William Joseph King. He lived to be 93 years old, and his mother lived to be a 103. He was born July 6, 1870 and he passed away in 1963. My goal is to beat both him and my great-grandmother, and at eighty-seven I am well on the way. He was bald-headed from the time he was 20 years of age. He had a very slight ring of hair just above his ears. He was a short man, probably about five feet six inches tall, but he was very strong. I can remember him telling that there was not a man around that he could not make wince as he grabbed and shook their hand. One piece of information that I did not have until my late teens was that he was an ex-convict. My mother told me one time that he was in prison for a year because of a charge of assault and battery. I can relate to him on that score. There is nothing more certain as when you hear the key click in the lock of your cell. I heard it very strongly in July 1952. There are two things that I vividly remember about him.

The first is that he was a very capable mason. He had a property that had sand stones on it that were as big as a house. I know because I saw them. He would take steel wedges and a good sledge hammer as he cut out stones for the retaining wall that goes down the East Hill into Brookville, Pennsylvania. In 1934 and 1935 I walked up and down that hill many times and I was told the story by my mother. Granddad took me up on the east hill of his property and had me help him by getting the right wedge, hammers, and other tools. I can remember trucks that would come and load up the stones that were cut and take them down to put on the retaining wall.

The second thing that I can vividly remember was that he loved gardening. He had three rows of garden about ten feet across that stretched about 200 feet long. That is 600 feet of lettuce, onions and all kinds of vegetables. About every 25 feet there was a path to cut the length down and make it easier to weed and work. That is a lot of weeding. I know, for I was taught how to do gardening. I love gardening even today. The weeding, not so much, but it has to be done.

As I write, the above encourages me to find out more about them, and, at the same time, find out who I am because of them. I have photos of my grandfathers and I know that I look like my paternal grandfather.

I made a discovery: the word "grandfather" is not mentioned in the Bible. The word "grandmother" is mentioned only once in 2 Timothy 1:5. However, I find in Matthew's genealogy of Jesus Christ that His paternal grandfathers name was Jacob (Matthew 1:16, NKJV). Matthew 1:1 reads, **"This is a record of the ancestors of Jesus the Messiah, a descendant of David and of Abraham."** It is amazing that the Christ's genealogy goes back generations to the beginning of the nation of Israel, not just to His grandfather, Jacob.

My Grandmothers

Now, I come to two ladies that are as different as they possibly could be. My paternal Grandmother was Margrett Emma Haugh nee' Lowry Carr. She was born July 28, 1977 and passed May 25, 1937. She had had an operation for a vaginal tumor. I do not have any information as to when she and Frank Carr married. She was the kindest person that I believe I have ever met. I can never remember an unkind word from her to anyone. I can only remember of her once being in Church. She taught me how to love people, how to milk old Betsy the cow, how to take care of Fanny the dog out by the smoke house, and how to do gardening on the farm. I can remember picking peas and digging potatoes with her. I can remember that one night all that we had for supper was new potatoes and peas. It might be that I dug the potatoes and picked and shelled the peas that we ate that night. What a wonderful memory!

Her mother was Grandma Haugh. Her roots went back to Holland. Hence, Grandma used a few Dutch terms. One day she took some evaporated milk cans up to the Blacksmith shop. She wanted to sweat the tops off so that the cans could be used at the spring house to get cold water. I can hear her calling to me, "Billy go to the kitchen and bring me the ole butcha messa." (Pennsylvania Dutch). She did not have to ask me twice-- off I ran and had the correct implement for the job as she was building a fire in the forge. After we were done, she showed me how to put out the fire in the forge. She cleaned the cans out and we went across to the Spring House. I can still taste how sweet and cold the water was that summer afternoon.

One memory of Grandma was that one day she got struck by lightning during a severe storm. She had been standing in the kitchen door watching the storm. I can remember how concerned we were. She lost her voice and she could not talk for a few days. There was no going to the doctor way back then.

One thing I also remember was her gentleness. I am sure that each of the kids on the farm went away with the impression that he or she was her favorite. Two step cousins were a part of the scene, but, for whatever reason, we seldom played together. I know that my sister and I were her favorites! That is the impression I have even to this day.

My mother's mother, Louisa Jane Henry King, was almost the exact opposite. She was born July 3, 1875 and she passed away in July 1937 from a gallstone operation. She was a Christian through and through. She went to Church whenever the Church door was open. Rain or shine, she took her umbrella and off she went. You will remember the week that I spent with her following the second grade. She turned me out into the rain and I spent the summer with my Uncle Frank and Aunt Huldah. I can remember my mother saying many times, "I do not know how she can be a Christian and still be as mean as she is." Only mother used more colorful language than I permit myself to use in this book. Again two things stick out as far as Grandma was concerned. First, it was through her that I was strengthened in my Christian faith. I praise God for knowing her. I wish I could go back and ask her forgiveness for calling her my bulldog Grandma. I am thankful that she showed a great example to a grandson that practices her church ethic to this day. You do not miss unless you are too sick to get out of bed. I am thankful to God for her faithfulness that has rubbed off on me.

The second thing that is important to me was that she taught me how to grow flowers. She had a bed of flowers about 20 feet across the bed for 200 feet. She taught me how to plant May pinks, azaleas, and all kinds of flowers. She taught me how to weed and make them things of beauty. As I went to the laboratory to get blood work done this afternoon, I was amazed at some to the beautiful flower gardens and potted plants that decorated homes along the way. Would I trade all these memories for other memories that might be a little different? No, I am the sum total of all the memories and things that happened to me as I was growing into manhood.

As I close, I read Psalm 139: and Praise God for the fact of the wonderful heritage that is mine. **And, "I will praise God. For I am fearfully and wonderfully made; marvelous are your works, and that my soul knows very well." (Psalm 139:14 NKJV)** *Father, I thank you for the Grandparents and parents that you ordained for me. Amen!*

Sharing With Sisters

I came from a family of seven siblings and one foster brother. My oldest sister was born on October 28, 1924. She lived about six hours and passed away. I do not know the reason for sure. My mother told me that she had problems giving birth and the doctor said she was a blue baby. An aunt made her a small casket and my father took her and buried her in the family plot.

On October 25, 1926, I was born during a snow storm on a Monday morning. I was delivered by the midwife before the doctor was able to arrive because of the storm. He pronounced that I was a whopping four pounds and four ounces and that I was doing just fine. Today, nearly 88 years later I am doing fine.

My sister Kathryn Lorraine was born July 15, 1928, at a formidable eleven pounds. She and I were always about the same size, but she was just a little bit ahead of me until my later teen years. There were two things that were true about us. The first was that we loved each other. Don't get between us. We took care of each other. The other is the fact that we loved to pick fights with each other and we did, often. This continued throughout our lives. We enjoyed each other. Lorraine would holler even if I sent her a letter. There was always something wrong with it. This continued until about ten years ago when she passed away from Alzheimer's disease.

My sister Edith Cecelia was born July 16, 1935. We were never really close. Lorraine helped mother take care of her. She was and is red headed. I left for the United States Navy when she was nine years old and we never got to know each other until later years, and part of the reason was that she married and has lived in Tennessee. Today, whenever we get on the phone we do not let any grass grow under our feet.

I had two brothers. James Wilson was born January 9, 1937. He had a brain defect and died about a half hour after birth. Robert Clyde was born November 4, 1941. Likewise, he was born with a brain defect and was stillborn. I am not sure of the medical reason for their deaths.

Gloria Jane, my youngest sister, was born June 10, 1945. Because of the two previous difficulties the doctor took no chances. Mother arrived at the clinic to give birth and while they were preparing everything for labor and delivery, she was born on the gurney. Mother told them she was ready, but before they were ready she was born. She was a beautiful baby girl.

I had a foster brother named Clyde^. He was born November 7, 1918. He lived with us for about 12 years. He served his country following the Attack on Pearl Harbor until he was about 25 years old. He eventually got married and moved to California. He had four children. The last time I heard about him was from his wife, in 2000. She told me that he had passed from diabetes.

As I look over the above list of brothers and sisters. I can feel the sorrow that was my mother's as she lost three children. However, I cannot even imagine what my father went through as he went out on cold days and laid a daughter and two sons to rest in our family plot. Tears whelm in my eyes just to think about it. Edith, Gloria, and I are all that have survived from our immediate family. However, God has richly blessed us with nephews and nieces like you could hardly believe. I can't count all that call me 'Uncle Bill.'

I would like to close this with a verse I found in 1 Peter 3:8. **"Finally, all of you should be of one mind. Sympathize with each other. Love each others as brothers and sisters. Be tenderhearted, and keep a humble attitude."** (NLT) *Father, may this verse ever be in our relationships with each other as each of us live out our days in your presence. Amen!*

High School Years

This section, having to do with my high school years, will take us from April 24, 1941 unto August 13, 1944. You will see transition from a country boy in Jefferson County, Pennsylvania to a city guy that puts roots down in Bradford, Pennsylvania and eventually joins the United States Navy. Can you imagine going from one room for 40 students in grades five through eight to junior high with a home room teacher, different rooms for each subject, and about 30 students in each classroom?

This was after an eventful 1941 summer. I was able to a get a job doing gardening and landscaping for a rich lady that had over three acres of lawn and beautiful shrubs. It probably helped that my dad was working for her husband in the oil fields. I had about three acres of lawn to mow by hand. There were flower beds galore, a gazebo that straddled a small rivulet of a creek, and absolutely no weeds allowed. On the back of the property, her son, John, had a cabin and a shed where he housed a steer. The steer had run into rough times. My daily chore was to clean the maggots from the base of his horns and to put tar on them so that flies would not bother him. Also, I was to make sure he had water and feed. By the end of the summer, the steer was healed and we were friends. Just before junior high school began in the fall, my family and I went back south to Brookville to visit. I can remember my father telling some friends how proud he was of me. I received a dollar an hour. This meant that I could buy my own school clothes. I was growing into a man.

You must remember that this country boy had never had electric lights; we used kerosene lamps. We had no inside plumbing, but an outhouse that was stinky in the summer and very cold in the winter. We had no telephone or radio. I am sure you cannot imagine life without all these amenities. But, to those of us who came out of the Great Depression, it was just the way life was. I can remember Mother buying a table model RCA radio. I believe it was the day that she purchased it that I managed to drop it while she was in town. The plastic case was broken in several pieces. Before she got home I had it glued together. It still worked and we had the glued table model years later. Now, it's a lovely memory. Then, it wasn't so pleasant.

Shortly after moving to Bradford, my father was able to rent a house on Big Shanty Road that led down the hill to Lewis Run and Bradford, Pennsylvania. We needed to take the bus to Bradford Junior High School, which was about fifteen miles away. My homeroom teacher was Miss Velma Chapman^. She was a small woman, and a very strict algebra teacher. I liked her and her class, where I became a friend to James^. We both excelled in algebra. She permitted the two of us to have adjoining seats in the back of the room so we could study independently of the other members of the class. We were both oddballs of sorts, and we clicked together. We rode the same school bus, which helped to develop our friendship. I also remember Mrs. Davidson's Latin Class during my freshman year. While Miss Chapman was diminutive, Mrs. Davidson was a tall woman. On occasions when I run across a Latin phrase in my study or research, I am amazed that I am able to understand and to translate after 70 years.

The next year I went to Bradford Senior High School. I took geometry and trigonometry in my sophomore and junior years, and I was scheduled to take calculus during my senior year, but I never made it because of my entry into the United States Navy. I was also enrolled in machine shop for the two years that I was a student at the senior high school. I had two classes that have helped me throughout my life. The first was Mr. Callahan's mechanical drawing class. I can still draw and read a blueprint and I can visualize what something will look like just by reviewing the plans. The second class was Miss Beyer's typing club. I am using that skill at the present time.

There were two classes that I did not exactly like. The first was gym, or athletics. Climbing a rope was one activity that I had to do, and I hardly ever got off the ground. The other was social studies. I will say that over the years, I have developed that area of academia until I can follow the political arena and make wise decisions. I might tell you that my grades in any case where not all that shabby. The machine shop, however, left its mark on me. Early on in my sophomore year, I dropped a lead hammer on my right big toe, and that toe has never been right since that occurrence.

I had one girlfriend during high school, named Janet Storms^. I took her to a movie once near the end of my junior year. The only problem was that I had to take my mother along with me because my mother could not drive, and she needed to go into town. Our family had only one vehicle. Our relationship was part of a pattern that you might like to know about. She was a senior that year, and therefore older than I was. You may be interested to know that I have never dated or been serious with a woman who was younger than me at any time in my life. I may have taken out some women who were younger than me, but it was only on rare occasions that this happened. It would be while I was in the Navy and I would go to a dance or activity at the USO (United Service Organization) for military men and women. Young girls would go to the USO to dance, to play games, to eat, and to help out the war effort by meeting military men. It helped us to forget home.

You will be interested to know that I have only graduated from the ninth grade. I have a certificate to prove my academic skill. The reason that I did not complete my senior year was that they were drafting men into the United States Army as soon as they turned 18. Some of my friends had this happen to them during their senior year. I decided that I wanted to join the United States Navy, and I enlisted on July 27th, 1944. I reported to the Federal Building in Buffalo, New York on August 14th and was sworn into the Navy on the 15th. They transported us to the Sampson United States Naval Training Base on Seneca Lake, New York, which was not too far from Geneva, New York. During my high school years, I lived a straight life most of time. I was not deeply involved in the gay lifestyle, apart from an occasional encounter. I pray that you are able to envision my life a little better than you have heretofore.

Summer Activities

It's always hard to wait until the school year ends and summer recess begins. I can never remember having a vacation anytime in my life while going to school. I might have gone to visit a family member on Sunday afternoon or having a family or friend or neighbor drop by, but there was never an extended week's vacation. Sunday afternoons were reserved for walks in the woods to hunt for flowers or berries. Even on Sundays, I had morning and evening chores. During most of my school years, we had a garden and animals to take care of. On the farm, we had horses, cows, chickens, pigs, dogs, and cats, and they all had to be fed. In many instances they became my friends. I can remember naming the rooster "Bill." I had to make sure to watch him or he would flog me, and his spurs hurt. Sally the pig weighed about 600 pounds. She had thirteen piglets in her first litter.

During high school, when we lived on Songbird Road near Custer City, Pennsylvania, we had this menagerie. We raised rabbits, turkeys, chickens and goats. I had to help with the chores during the school year, and during summer they became my responsibility. Besides caring for the animals, there was always the garden that had to be planted, weeded and harvested. Dad and I planted, I weeded and tilled it, and I helped harvest all kinds of vegetables. I can't remember planting spinach, but I do remember having to take care of kale, squash, and cucumbers and shelling peas, and snapping beans, and helping mother can tomatoes. I was busy. In July, we started picking blue and blackberries. Are you tired yet?

During my sophomore and Junior years, I had a job at the New Bradford Theatre as an usher. There were three of us that had jobs at the theater: Bill, Bud*, and Bob. Bob would eventually become my brother-in-law, and we are friends to this day. Our parents would usually take us to work, but there were those times when we had to hitchhike or walk home. It was eight miles from the theatre to my home, and we had to be there every Tuesday and Thursday night. They had bingo during intermissions, and we were expected to read the cards when anyone cried "Bingo!" and to deliver the prize. We wore formal attire: black pants with a red stripe down the leg, a white dickey with a black bow tie, and a red waist length jacket that was tight fitting. We called them "monkey suits."

There was free time, believe it or not. My father worked in the oil fields and there were times when we would go with him. The garden was forgotten as we learned new skills that would eventually lead to us working as tool dressers or roustabouts in the oil fields. This was true of all three. Bob and I still chuckle about our experiences together. The one thing that he did alone was his paper route.

There were other days when we had nothing to do. If we asked nicely, someone might take us to the fresh water pond that was cold all year long for some swimming. They had these man-made pools on the leases to have fire protection and a supply of water where needed for steam boilers and other necessities. One thing I can say is that we were not bored during the summer while waiting for school to start again. We could hardly wait for the day after Labor Day.

Athletics and I never clicked. Bob played football, so I had to go to football games to see him and another friend, Gene, play. I can remember that one of my friends, Wallace^, got hurt at one of the games. I offered to drive him in my Dad's car, but went over the bank along the road, and they had to push me out so I could take him to the hospital. My Dad never found out, and I never told him.

My Father taught me how to drive. That was a nervous experience for him. I was all over the road, much to his consternation. I had to take my driver's test three times before passing. The first time, the State Police Office told me, "Be sure and make up your mind about what to do and do it." I do not remember what happened the second time, but the third time I passed. I had a job by then at Dresser's Manufacturing Company in the half-track department, forming Army half-track wheels as part of the war effort, on a "Victory Shift". I asked Dad, "Can I drive myself to work?" He allowed me to take his car. I drove into the parking lot and promptly ran the right front fender into the parking rails. Dad was not too happy. A couple of days later, he ran the same fender into a six-inch pipe in our garage. He loved his Chevrolet car and got it fixed so it looked brand spanking new. About two weeks later, he did the same thing again. He never got it fixed again. It was that way until he got another car. Myke, this reminds me of the hassle that we had over parallel parking when you were going to take your test. You were so upset that you had Mom do the honors, and you passed your test. Aren't these great memories? I am sure that whoever reads this will agree. I know that I never lacked something to do in my youth.

PART THREE: ADULTHOOD

My adult life was marked by two things: Navy life and family life. I proudly served in the United States Navy from August 14, 1944 to December 22, 1952, and I would serve again if I was given the opportunity. Age is a factor. I stood on the Northern Tip of Ireland on May 13, 2009 and looked out to the North Sea. I remembered the lift of the sea and the roll, the pitch, and the spray hitting me in the face as I manned the Polaris. My daughter, Sandra, had a cut glass portrait of "The Old Man of the Sea". An aged seaman is standing with his back to the viewer, wearing an old sailor's cap on his head. A young boy stands at his knee, dressed in a new boy's sailor suit with his back to the viewer. You can see the waves tossing as they look out to sea. It gives me a nostalgic vision. I remember the Navy bases. I can feel the decks of the USS LST 971, the USS Reuben James DE 153, USS Cocopa ATF 101, and the USS Timmerman EDD 828 rise under my feet in memory. The only vessel, of those named, still in service is the USS Cocopa, which was sold to Mexico and renamed. I remember the men that I sailed with. Many were great sailors and friends. All I can do at 87 is to look and to reminisce.

Another major part of life after high school was my journey as a husband to four different women and as a father to seven children. Ecclesiastes 9:9 reads, **"Live joyfully with the wife whom thou lovest."**
The text is sometimes misquoted to read, "Live joyfully with the wife of your youth." I want to use that quotation here. I am very glad that that I never had four wives to deal with as the patriarch Jacob did all at one time. My four wives have been consecutive. I have often thought, "Which one would I choose to be with if I was confronted with that choice today?" I am thankful that I will never have to make that choice, because Jesus told us, **"For in the resurrection they are neither married nor given in marriage, but are like the angels of God in Heaven."** (Matthew 22:30 NKJV)

Along with the blessing of four wives came the blessing of many children. Psalm 127:3-5 in the New King James Version has this to say about progeny:" **Behold, children are a heritage from the Lord, the fruit of the womb is a reward. Like arrows in the hand of a warrior, so are the children of one's youth. Happy is the man who has his quiver full of them; they shall not be ashamed,**
but shall speak with their enemies in the gate." I have often wondered how many are in a quiver. It depends on how big is your quiver. I have heard thirteen. I looked on Google and found five. I do not know. I have wondered what my inheritance will be to my "Children." My inheritance will be found in them. In Biblical days, it was wealth to have children when you faced the enemy at the gate. The more there were, the better you were when things were going wrong. **"They shall speak with the enemy in the gate."**

Money comes and goes. My children have increased and will continue to increase. (This includes extended family) My prayer is that they might live lives that glorify my God. Amen.

A Letter to Myke

Dear Myke,

I arrived at Sampson United States Naval Training Center on August 15, 1944 for boot camp. I was one of 106 men in Company (Co) 246. The Commanding Officer was Richard Biquist, Al Frasca was the Assistant Company Commander, and the Master at Arms (MAA) was Robert Manfredi. We were split into two platoons of 53 each. Let the competition begin.

The first thing that happened was that we had our naval clothes issued to us. We were required to send our civilian clothes and belongings home. The only things that we did not have to send home were our personal Bibles. We received dungarees, our white and blue uniforms. We were taught how to fold and secure them Navy style. For instance, handkerchiefs had to be folded in fours and rolled as tight as possible, and each piece of clothing had to be rolled and secured with clothes stops and tied with a square knot. A clothes stop was similar to a shoelace, but more on the order of clothes line material, except they were not as thick and about ten inches long. The entire issue had to be put in a sea bag. If you did not get it right the first time, you had to start the process all over again. The "Government Issue" (GI) included two blankets, a pillow, two mattress covers, two pillow cases, and a "Ditty bag" in which you kept your toilet articles and miscellaneous items. They issued you only what you needed to be a sailor, from dog tags to the finished Apprentice Seaman (AS), in Navy slang, a "Swabby". At first, it was hard, but once you got the hang of it you could be ready to go at a moment's notice.

Dad

Joy and Sorrow with the Wife of My Youth

I met my first wife, Marian Elizabeth Bradt, on a Friday near my 18th birthday. I had just completed boot camp in the United States Navy and was on my first leave. My father and mother were visiting mutual friends on Washington Street in Bradford, Pennsylvania, and I dropped in where they were visiting. They may have planned it; however I was never aware of any such plans. I visited with Dad, Mom, our friends, and "Bradt". (All of her friends called her by her last name.) We made arrangements to visit her parents, Carl and Holice, the next day in Eldred, Pennsylvania. Around 10:30 P.M. my father and mother decided to leave, and their friends retired for the evening. I know that I, and I believe Bradt did as well, realized it was "love at first sight". We confirmed our feelings. My whites gave proof to my parents as to my activity that evening. I cleaned them the best I could, and my mother helped me get them in a suitable condition to return to naval duty. After returning to base, Bradt wrote me a note informing that she had miscarried. I came home on leave, April, 1945, and our feelings were strengthened for each other during that time together.

The letters flew between her and me after I returned to the base and eventually boarded ship. I am not sure how long we had to hurry up and wait, but it was probably about a week until I left for Radar School at Fort Lauderdale, Florida. We took a bus, and about the time we got near Philadelphia, Pennsylvania, they stopped and took me off and sent me to the U.S. Naval Hospital with the measles. I missed my assignment. I arrived the next week and was in a new company where I had to make all new friends.

Did I say "hurry up and wait?" That is what happened upon graduating from Radar School. Around Thanksgiving 1944, it was off to the U.S. Naval Amphibious Base in Little Creek, Virginia. This was an experience. The base had only been in service since 1942, and it was built on converted swamp and farm land. They billeted you in either Quonset huts or tents. I was a lucky one who pulled a tent. Remember, this was in November and December when it was cold and damp. Two blankets and an oil stove in the center of the tent were used at night to keep you warm. During the day, while we were training, the stove would go out. It was *cold*.

I was granted a Christmas leave that year, so I came home and married Marian on December 22, 1945, at the Wesleyan Methodist Church in Bradford, PA. She had managed somehow to get the paperwork completed for our marriage. On Sunday, December 25, at about 8:00 A.M., I boarded a train to go back to ship. After returning to ship, it was not long before I received the great news that we were to have a child. Mail really flew from then on until I was discharged on July 5, 1946. Around Christmas time, I was shipped to the US Naval Receiving Station in Boston, Massachusetts to join the crew for the USS LST 971. We were at the receiving station for both Christmas and New Years. Early in January 1945, the crew went aboard ship, and it was commissioned on January 15th. We immediately went on shake down in the *very* choppy North Atlantic. I was a part of the commissioning ceremony and shake down. It was a great experience. They told us later that at one time we had taken a 44 degree roll. Forty-six would have been bad news. When we got back from shake down, we were immediately decommissioned on January 29th. The ship was to be taken to Baltimore, Maryland to be reworked and commissioned the USS Menelaus ARL 13.

The crew left the ship and was immediately reassigned. This was no mean feat. The crew was composed of 232 enlisted personnel and 13 officers. I was immediately slated for Landing Craft Infantry and transferred to Staten Island for training. The LCI's were 153 feet in length and 23.25 feet at the beam. They normally would have a ships compliment of about 60 sailors on board. The LCI's were used for transporting the US Army Infantry and US Marines (about 200 strong) onto beaches for invasions. While I was stationed on Staten Island, I was given a week's additional Radar School in how to do minor maintenance. No electronics technicians were aboard the LCI.

I can remember that they took us to one of the docks on Staten Island where we had an abandon ship drill off of a 40-foot high pier into the water. Amazingly, I survived. I was sent to New Orleans for further training, but that was cancelled and I was instead transferred to the US Naval Yard at Houston, Texas to become a part of the crew of the USS Reuben James, Destroyer Escort DE 153. I boarded her in November 1945, and they immediately home ported us to Norfolk, Virginia. The Reuben James was used to escort vessels in the Atlantic. It was ironic that we seemed to normally operate south of Newfoundland in the winter months and return to Norfolk and to operate in the Caribbean in the summer. While in the Caribbean, we used the US Naval Base at Guantanamo, Cuba as our port of call, and in the North Atlantic we used the Portsmouth Naval Shipyard as our port of call.

The USS Reuben James was 306 feet in length with a beam of 37 feet and a draft of 13.5 feet. The ship had a crew of about 213 officers and men aboard. I can remember one escort mission that we had. We and about three other destroyers and destroyer escorts were assigned to an Escort Carrier (CVE) Task Force. A carrier escort is a "baby flat top". The Commodore on the flat top decided to have a pilot exercise. He ordered planes off the flight deck when you could see the screws coming out of the water. We lost three planes that day, but they were able to rescue the pilots. The USS Reuben James' mission was to protect the flat top directly from the rear. From that point of view, it was a success. I am sure he had to explain about the loss of three planes.

I earned Petty Officer 3rd Class, Radar Man 3rd Class (RD3), while I was on board the James, and additionally I was asked to be the ship's Post Master. The former mailman was transferred and they needed someone to receive, sort, and deliver the mail aboard ship. It was a good assignment for me. If we had to anchor in the harbor, I had to be ready to get on board the captain's gig to go to the Carrier Escort (CVE) to get the mail, or if we docked, I had to get the mail from the naval facility. This included money orders, stamps, etc. I have learned many times that I work best in that kind of situation. I can lead, but I am better at being further down the line a little bit. That way I do not make as many mistakes. I have found that all throughout my life, I am better at being second than first.

On Victory in Europe Day, on May 8th 1945, the Germans surrendered to the Allied Forces on President Harry Truman's 61st birthday. He declared it was the best birthday present he had ever received. The President announced the surrender to the United States and dedicated the day to President Franklin Delano Roosevelt who had died on April 12th less than a month before the surrender. There was a major shift in the Japanese conflict. That theater would wind down on August 14th with the signing of the "Final Unconditional Surrender" aboard the battleship the USS Missouri BB 63 in Tokyo Harbor on September 2nd with General of the Armies Douglas MacArthur signing for the United States and a Japanese delegation signing for Japan. The Navy did not need all of us.

I was transferred from the USS Reuben James near the end of June 1946 for separation. I received an honorable discharge from the Navy on July 5, 1946. Upon my arrival home, my wife Marian and I set up housekeeping at 13 Chestnut Street in Bradford, Pennsylvania. It was a small one-bedroom apartment with a shared bathroom, but it was home. Life in the apartment was fun. Marian and I were getting to know each other. She was an excellent cook. I do not know how to explain why I remember that one evening we had plain boiled potatoes and hamburger. What we had for vegetables and dessert that evening has long since slipped my memory, but it was special.

I was able to obtain work at the Kendall Refining Company as a yard worker. We cleaned all kinds of tanks that had oil and gasoline in them, or if there was a leak in an oil line, we dug it up and repaired it. One time, I helped dig a crater about 20 feet deep to repair a large gas line with brass tools to prevent sparks.

My wife visited her Obstetrics Doctor on August 27th 1946. He told her that she had to quit eating potatoes and salt because she had too much fluid in her system. We could handle that, since she was a nurse. However, on Thursday morning while I was at work, my parents stopped by and they decided to take her to Bradford Hospital. At noon, my father picked me up at the Kendall Refining Company, since she was in critical condition. The doctor decided that they would have to take the baby on Friday the 30th by Cesarean section to save both hers and the baby's life, even though the pregnancy was about four weeks short of being full term. On Friday August 30th at 12:15 PM, the baby was delivered. She had three close friends from her nursing class who were with her all the rest of the day. She was in such a good condition that they and my parents took off for a dance. The nurse asked me to leave the room just about 8:00 P.M. My cigarette was just half-finished when she hurriedly called me back to the room. I walked into Marian's room in time to see her pass away at 8:15 P.M.

I was unable to contact my parents. There were no cell phones in those days, and I had no transportation. Marian had picked out the name for the baby: Sandra Elaine. I named the baby, and as I was not able to get a hold of my parents, I walked about two miles to Grandma Inscho's on Kendall Ave. They had gone with them dancing. It was a shock both to my family and also for Bradt's nursing friends. They had left feeling everything was alright and that there were not going to be any problems, and when they came back, they intended to special her during the morning shift (11 P.M. to 7 A.M.). They found out that she had passed away.

I was in a daze during the next several days. I can remember my father taking me to get a suit for the funeral. I can remember her lying in state at the funeral home in Bradford. The room was lined with flowers. People flocked to see her. On Monday, we had the funeral service at her Grandmother Cooley's^ on Mechanic Street in Eldred, PA. All I remember of that service is that the preacher, Rev. David Anderson, who had married us, preached about sunlight. I would like to have had a copy of that sermon. It would undoubtedly have a greater meaning today than it did on that day.

Following the funeral I moved in with my parents up on Songbird Road in Custer City, Pennsylvania. Sandy came home from the hospital and mother helped me take care of her. For the first few months, Sandy had colic all the time. The only way that she could get any sleep at night was lying on her tummy on my chest. Even now, as I look back, it seems like a dream. My first marriage ended after eight months and nine days. I was not 20 at the time.

My mother later told me that she and Bradt had talked. Both of us were nominal Christians. We read our Bibles regularly. Mom had asked her what would happen if God should call us to the mission field. She had said, "We will go."

Father, I thank You for the precious memories; that are a part of my life as I remember the wife of my youth. Amen!

Losing Control

I continued to work at the Kendall Refinery, but I asked for and received assignment to the "Dubbs Crew." The crew consisted of eight men and one foreman. The Dubbs was a cracking process that produced petroleum products. The unit had two cracking towers about 10 feet in diameter and 40 feet high. They were filled with oil or pitch-tar and heated under pressure to about 2500 degrees (F) to burn off impurities and to produce graphitization. The end product for our unit was a train car load of petroleum coke four times a week. The process was used to produce a high octane gasoline. The coke was used to make graphite for pencil lead and also to make nuclear rods. The crew was black with soot after unloading a tower. It was hot and dusty in the towers, and we had to use petroleum jelly just to keep the coke dust away from our eyes. To offset this was the fact that we worked about five hours and got full pay for the day. This permitted us to leave no later than 1:30 PM unless a problem arose. Then, we worked until the problem was solved. On Thursdays, we went back for one day to being yard workers.

I did fine from that time until about the middle of January 1947. It could probably have been said, "I was the model father." But, that ended when one day in mid-January my friend, "Bud" R. Gordio ^, with whom I worked, asked me to go on a date with him and his sister Teetie. I went on the date and for the next nine months we went to ball games, bars, drinking, bowling, dancing or anything else that caught our fancy. I managed to be home with my daughter and my parents for about three days during that nine-month period.

I dated Teetie and I am unable to recall her given name. She was a great dancing partner. We cleared the floor many times during the "Jitter Bug" dance craze that followed the end of World War II in the late forties. We dated casually and there was some talk of getting married. I can remember only one time that we ever had a date and were not accompanied by someone else. The date turned out uneventful. Bud's parents lived together but slept in separate rooms. Teetie always slept in her mother's room and I shared Bud's room and bed. It was not the greatest scenario for a budding romance.

The thing that helped straighten the situation out was that one night I had my Father's car and was going home from Bud's. I had been drinking, and I fell asleep and took a tree out in a farmer's pasture. I was in no condition to walk and had no way to get home, so I crawled back into the car and went to sleep. Sometime during the early morning hours, my dad came looking for me and he told me in no uncertain terms what he was going to do if I ever did that again. He noted that the car could have caught on fire and that I needed to come home and take care of my daughter. I moved back home the first week of September 1947.

How I met Valerie^ is a mystery to me that I have no way to solve. It may have been in a bar or dancing with my parents. I do not know. She looked a lot like my first wife in nearly every way and that was a plus. We were married October 25, 1947, on my 21st birthday. My best man asked me this question on the way to Valerie's and my wedding: "Is it tail-light or love-light?" I know that I mumbled, "Love-light".

We lived in my parent's home with my daughter, entertaining the idea that it only would be until we could get our own place. Early in January 1948, we came to the end of our marriage. We were out visiting some of her family in the area. We came home and she was putting Sandra to bed when she misused her by severely spanking her. My daughter was fourteen months old at the time. I spoke to her, and she responded, "At least I did not take a knife to her." [Note: there had been two recent instances in the community where that had happened to children.]

Needless to say, I went berserk. As I look back, if it had not been for my father responding to the situation, I would have done her real harm. As it was, I told her as we went to bed, "If you are here tomorrow night when I come home from work; I will throw you out the nearest opening." I got up and went to work the next day, and I have not seen nor have I had any personal contact with her from that day until this day. I learned later from several of my friends that she had approached them for extramarital personal favors. On the other hand, I was approaching the same male friends for personal favors as well. Our divorce became final June 16, 1948.

Following our divorce, I continued working the same type of schedule, but there was a twist. I got a maroon 1940 Pontiac. Now that I had transportation, I went out with about six of the crew on a regular basis. The other three were happily married, and they went home when they were supposed to. Lionel^, a bar friend, and I would get together intermittently. On at least one occasion, I took four of the crew out at one time. I was prostituting myself.

I would be considered bi-sexual today. As I look back on that period of my life I would say that I was about forty percent heterosexual and about sixty percent gay. I was an alcoholic. I drank because I had a problem, and because I had a problem, I drank. It would be four years before I returned to US Naval duty on December 10th 1950, and it was the same thing over and over again. The following scripture describes my life at that time almost to the letter. Needless to say, "I needed help."

1 Timothy 1:8-10 (NKJV)

But we know that the law *is* good if one uses it lawfully, ⁹ knowing this: that the law is not made for a righteous person, but for *the* lawless and insubordinate, for *the* ungodly and for sinners, for *the* unholy and profane, for murderers of fathers and murderers of mothers, for manslayers, ¹⁰ for fornicators, for sodomites, for kidnappers, for liars, for perjurers, and if there is any other thing that is contrary to sound doctrine.

I decided that I needed to do something about it. I chose to apply for sea duty. At least there would be no drinking at sea. I thought that would help, and in a strange way, it did.

Naval Tour Pacific

I realized my dilemma. I knew that I needed to get away from drinking and the situation in which I was caught up. My solution was to go back into active duty in the Navy and ask for sea duty. I applied for sea duty with the Bureau of Naval Operations. They did not serve alcohol on most of the ships in 1951. In late November 1950, my family had a going away party for me as I was to report to active duty on December 10, 1950. We were eating and partying with a keg of beer on hand. At the party, my oldest sister Lorraine took me aside and told me, "Bill you need to quit drinking. Why don't you go to some AA meetings? They would help you! And, please start going to church." She told me that she and her husband had started to go to the Free Methodist Church in their village and that they had been saved on April Fool's Day in 1950. She continued, "It was no joke, it works!" She ended by saying that she would be praying for me. What she said that night still rings in my ears. In my mind's eye and in my being I can still hear her talking with me. It was too late. I had to report for active duty. Later, you will find out how long she prayed before her prayers were answered.

I cannot remember where I reported to. However, I ended up at the Naval Base in San Diego. I was targeted to join the ship's crew of the USS Cocopa, ATF 101. The ATF stands for Auxiliary Fleet Tug. The Cocopa was 205 feet long, 38.5 feet at the beam, and had a draft of 15.3 feet. We had a compliment of 77 according to a picture I have of the crew. This included four commissioned officers, and three Petty Officers. We were home ported in San Diego, but that did not last long. We were soon on our way to Honolulu, Hawaii, where we were home ported for 1951.

Diamond Head and Pearl Harbor were sights to behold. I remember them as I was on Radar and Quartermaster duty as we approached the Islands of Hawaii. As part of the bridge gang, I was assigned responsibility for the chart room. Each time we entered port, it was my task to update all the charts in the chart room. Obsolete charts had to be taken out of the files and destroyed or discarded, and new charts were inserted in their place. I enjoyed being on the radar and at the same time taking care of the chart room. I was responsible to the Chief Petty Officer of Communications.

The first salvage job we did was to go to the East Coast of Kauai, and latch onto an oil tanker/freighter. The freighter had run aground on some volcanic reef and was about to break up. I cannot remember her name. Our assignment was to hitch onto her and prevent her from going further aground. You will note that a ship is always referred to as a "her" in naval terminology. There was oil every place on board the freighter and also on our ship and on nearly everyone of the ship's crew. The officers were not exempt. When our job was finished, it was back to Pearl Harbor to clean up. We no sooner had the USS Cocopa cleaned up when our home port was changed to Apra Harbor, Guam for six months. As near as I can determine, Guam is about 3000 nautical miles from Pearl Harbor.

We had not been at Guam too long when we were off to the Anatahan Island to accept the final surrender of Japanese holdouts that were on the Island. The following is a report found on wikipedia of the action:

"The AP reported on June 27, 1951 that a Japanese petty officer who surrendered on Anatahan Island in the Marianas two weeks before said that there were 18 other holdouts there. A U.S. Navy plane had flown over the island and he spotted 18 Japanese soldiers on a beach waving white flags.[9] However, the Navy remained cautious as the Japanese petty officer had warned that the soldiers were "well-armed and that some of them threatened to kill anyone who tried to give himself up. The leaders profess to believe that the war is still on." The Navy dispatched, a seagoing tug, the Cocopa, to the island in hopes of picking up some or all of the soldiers without incident." The actual count was 19 holdouts. What the article did not say was that the Island and the holdouts were infested with flies. And, the lack of fresh water was very apparent. As they came aboard the Cocopa the flies came with them. They were feed on the stern of the ship and as much as we could, they were given clean clothes."[2]

One thing that is of interest is that an ocean going tug is a working vessel. They are used for salvage, for towing barrages, and for towing larger naval vessels from one port to another when necessary. You need to know that the top speed of a tug is about 16.5 knots. However, when a tug is towing something, the speed is dependent not only on the size of the towed object, but also on sea conditions. At times you can be down to 2 or 3 knots. During the time I was aboard the Cocopa, we travelled approximately a total of 25,000 nautical miles. The earth's circumference is 24,860 miles measured through the poles.

I have taken the time to figure out the distance we travelled during 1951 and early 1952. The distance from San Diego to Pearl Harbor is roughly 4055 miles. From Pearl Harbor to Guam was 3000 miles. From Guam to Anatahan Island was 400 miles round trip, and from Guam to the Palau Island was 1200 miles round trip. From Guam to Naha, Okinawa was 2826 miles round trip. We towed a barge to the Palau Islands. I went ashore in the Palau Islands with a Philippine friend, Eceja. We came across a Philippine restaurant where the cook served us and we enjoyed turtle steak. We had state-side beer while we waited for our steak. That was the first and only time I have ever eaten turtle.

We no sooner arrived at our home port in Guam than we were en route to Naha, Okinawa for a month. I do not remember if we were towing or not. One thing I do remember is that after I arrived, I met a young lady by the name of Osukasama. She never spelled it for me, but she did tell me that her name meant "Bright Moon," and I guess I was a little moonstruck. I do know that for the month that we were at port of call in Naha, Okinawa, my time off ship was brightened. I remember that one evening while eating in a home in Naha, we were served a Japanese meal. I learned later that the meat was cat. That was the first and only time that I have ever eaten cat.

We returned from Naha, Okinawa to Apra Harbor, Guam, our home port. Our home port was about to be changed, but first we had time for liberty

---

[2] (2014). Japanese holdout. *Wikipedia.* Retrieved from http://en.wikipedia.org/wiki/Japanese_holdout on 14 September 2014.

in Guam. The difference between "liberty" and "leave" is primarily time. Liberty is for the evening or the weekend, while leave is for an extended period of time. Leave would probably be termed today "rest and relaxation". One night, about eight of us decided to go into a nearby village. We had no transportation. We hitchhiked. We were able to receive a ride with a bunch of Navy Sea Bees, in a pickup truck. The truck was loaded. They had as many Sea Bees as we had Navy. We were stuffed into the bed, which had a cover over it. So far, so good! However, after a few beers here and there, once again we met up with them and to base we went. But, as we jumped out of the back of the pickup, they jumped out after us. What a ruckus that was. I ended up with a camera as my prize. I still have pictures of the event after sixty odd years. Once in a while, I break those pictures out and I have a good chuckle.

It was not long until we were off to San Diego, CA our original home port, and having some repairs to the Tug. But, that was a long way to go. We went to Pearl Harbor, 3000 miles away, and checked in there until we received our orders. We were off to Pudget Sound Naval Shipyard near Bremerton, Washington. We were to pick up the USS Canberra CA 70 and tow her to the west side of the Panama Canal. She was a cruiser that was to be converted to a guided missile cruiser. She had been decommissioned and was slated to be converted at the New York Shipbuilders Corp. in Camden, New Jersey. This was January 4 1952. She would later be re-commissioned the USS Canberra CAG-2 on June 15 1956. The estimated time to get to the Panama Canal, 3075 nautical miles, was approximately a month at about four knots, depending on sea conditions. We were docked at the Panama Canal for about a month. During this time, we had liberty, and I availed myself of the opportunity frequently. I had established a relationship with a lady there. She took up my time, and I was not bored.

However, there were those long times out to sea. At least three of us had established a close relationship. We took liberty together when available, and we were tight aboard ship as well. One afternoon while in port at Guam, I was alone in the Chart Room. I had some time and I was writing a letter home to my mother. Suddenly, there was a knock at the hatch of the Chart Room. It was the Petty Officer MAA (Master at Arms). The MAA was charged with the security of the vessel at all times. He assured me that our area was secure. That was the first of many instances aboard ship. The three of us would go on liberty together, usually leaving separately, but we would always meet up later aboard ship, in a motel room, or whatever happened to come our way. Just prior to returning to the USS Cocopa, on Liberty one night, I went and got super drunk. I know I came back to ship, but that is all I know. No one would ever tell me what happened -- not even my best friend. I have no idea what occurred, and I can only imagine.

Finally, the ship left the Panama Canal and travelled to San Diego, the city that was once again designated our Home Port. The 2905 nautical miles took a lot less time going north than when we were going south. I am not sure of the extent of the repairs. However, I was given the task of updating all the charts after being to sea for about six months. I was about to be discharged. Security and Navy protocol was at low tide. I was dressed in dungarees and I had to take charts off the ship for disposal. The Petty Officer on duty at the gangplank did not like the fact that I could not salute the flag as I left the ship with my arms full of charts. He was slightly inebriated and he pulled his 45 and cocked it at me. My friend happened to come by and defused the situation. He talked me out of reporting it to the Captain or Executive Officer. Both of us were due for discharge the following week.

I was transferred from aboard ship to the US Naval Receiving Station, San Diego for discharge from the United States Naval Reserve. I was discharged March 28, 1952. My parents and family had kept the Christmas tree up since Christmas. When I got home, I was able to open my presents with my daughter Sandra. At this time, I cannot recall the events that brought me home on this occasion. I returned to active duty at the Naval Station in Brooklyn, New York on June 5, 1952, two months and eight days from the time I was discharged from San Diego.

As I look back, I hang my head in shame. I am sure that then I did not realize the anguish that I put my parents through, and today, tears well up in my eyes as I remember. They were taking care of my daughter and would continue to do so until December 22nd 1952. I never asked their forgiveness.

I wish that I could do so today, but I cannot. I have to look into the mirror of my life and say, "I do not like what I see. However, I forgive you." This reminds me of a passage in Colossians 3:12-16, and these words from verse thirteen, **"Forgiving one another … even as Christ forgave you, so you also must do."** I know that Christ forgave me. Therefore, I say to myself, "I forgive you." I must accept my forgiveness or I will continue in self-guilt. Today, I praise God for that gift of His Grace!

The Brig, and What I Learned There

I reported to the Brooklyn Navy Yard in New York on June 5th 1952 for active duty. It was not too long until I was assigned to the crew of the USS Timmerman, EDD 828 (Experimental), a vessel that was soon to be commissioned. The crew was being assembled at the US Naval Receiving Station in Boston, Massachusetts. I reported to Boston, and by early July I joined the ship's company that was forming for the Timmerman. She was 390.5 feet long, 41 feet at the beam, and she had a draft of 14 feet. She had an estimated speed of 40 to 43 knots. The compliment was composed of 336 officers and enlisted men. The "E" in her designation signified that she was experimental.

I had been in the crew for about two weeks when I met a man that I was interested in. One night I made a move. I got back to my rack, and in the meantime, he had contacted the Navy Shore Patrol (the same as Military Police) and put them on the lookout for someone suspicious. Most of the crew was on liberty, and I was taken into custody. The Shore Patrol immediately transferred me to the US Naval Brig and I was to occupy solitary Cell B-2-1. I can remember the sound of the SP's key turning in the lock that night. It's a sound I have never forgotten. I was there for about three weeks while they were investigating the situation.

While the investigation was going on, I was praying, "Lord get me out of this and I will serve you." In about three weeks I was returned to the ship's crew of the Timmerman. Never once in the weeks that followed did I go to church or keep my promise. Later, I was talking with the ship's clerk that took care of the crew's records and he asked me this question, "Bill, I have seen your records and you were as guilty as h*ll. How did you get out of it?" I do not think I replied to him. I know this. I did not go to any base worship services or church services.

What I did do was continue to get ready to put the USS Timmerman into commission on September 26, 1952. Also, we were getting her ready for shakedown. This normally means about two months' work on board the ship, cleaning her up and getting every area ready for sea trials. I was a part of that. I was also a part of nearly every liberty party that was available to me. I started to walk down Fargo Street toward the heart of Boston, and invariably I would get picked up by about four or five young men my age and we would spend the night drinking among other things. Essentially, I was prostituting myself. I went on liberty, I got drunk, and whatever happened was what was expected for the occasion. This activity continued until Saturday, October 25, 1952 -- my 26th birthday. That night I went out, and I do not know what happened on that liberty or what happened when I returned to the vessel. I was drunk and virtually passed out while still on my feet.

The next thing I know that happened was that on November 4th 1952 at noon, while I was in the chow line, the Naval Shore Patrol picked me out of the line, and it was back to the Boston Naval Brig, cell B-2-1, with no lunch. This was the day that General of the Armies, David D. Eisenhower was elected President of the United States. Believe me they had other cells. I lucked out the second time for that cell. At the Investigation by the Naval Officers (similar to the FBI), I was told that I had approached several of my shipmates and that they had reported me to the Ship's Executive Officer.

On November 18th a gay friend that was in General Population in the brig came over to visit with me in solitary at about 1900 hours. I could not believe that God would want me after all that I had done in my life. My idea was that you clean up your act and that God may save you. That was not the case. God wanted to save me, and the Holy Spirit would help me clean up my life. My friend had attended Providence Bible School in Rhode Island. He told me, "Bill, it has to be 100 percent faith. He gave me this analogy: "It can't be 99 44/100% like a bar of Ivory soap, it has to be the whole thing." Somehow, this made sense to me. I looked up to the back of B Block and I simply made this prayer, "Lord, help me to believe that you really want me." Do you know what? He did, and He still does! I have walked with my Lord since that date at 7:15 PM until now. It will be sixty-two years come November. That night, I read my Bible for the first time in years, and I prayed. I did not know what to pray. I found that it was hard to read, and I could not remember the

Lord's Prayer. I ended up that evening with this simple prayer on my lips and heart: "Lord, teach me to pray." He has been teaching me to pray for nigh onto 62 years.

It was about this same time that the Navy Investigator called me to his office and interrogated me. I admitted the truth through tears. I loved naval duty. However, that marked the beginning of the end for me. I signed papers that would let me out of the United States Navy with an "Other Than Honorable" discharge. Two things happened. The first was that I wrote to my father and asked him with an explanation, "May I come home?" He wrote back and said "Yes." Otherwise, I would have been on the street.

The other thing was that the Brig Shore Patrol asked me to take charge of the Gear Locker. In civilian terms, it was a utility room. I had to check out buckets, mops, brooms, and other cleaning supplies and make sure that I received them back and checked them in for security purposes. Also, I overheard two of the SP's conversing with one another. One said to the other, "Something has really happened to him."

I had made a bargain with the Lord that if anyone asked me about my reasons for getting out of the Navy, I would simply tell them. The first time that happened was when I was 52 years old. In 1978, a seventeen year old Catholic High School Student asked to interview me as a part of his Social Studies class. He knew how to conduct an interview. I gave him the basic facts, and he received an "A" plus for his grade. I have kept my bargain to this day. "Don't Ask, Don't Tell" is not in my vocabulary. I simply witness to what God in His love has accomplished in my life. What He has done in my life, I am sure that He can do in your life.

I was in the Navy for six months and eighteen days for my third enlistment, and I served approximately two months and eighteen days in prison. This is important to remember as it is just the beginning of what Jesus would eventually ask me to do for Him in regards to prison ministries.

The Start of Something Beautiful

My Christian life began on November 18, 1952 at 7:15 P.M. I have continued in integrity and faithfulness unabated unto the present. The first thing I did was start reading my Bible and praying daily. I was discharged from the US Naval service on December 22, 1952. That is a hot date for me. My first wife and I got married on that date, her mother died on that date (I had her funeral on Christmas Day), my oldest sister died on that date, and last year I was discharged from the hospital on that date. My medical condition has been such that I have had to live with my son Bill Jr. since then. When that date comes near, I try not to dwell on it.

Prior to my discharge, while I was still in the brig, I went each Sunday to the chaplain's worship service. I still remember the second sermon I heard: "Second Choices". The sermon was based on Acts 16, in which the Apostle Paul had to make choices under the guidance of the Holy Spirit. He chose to accept the "Macedonian Call." Since the Apostle accepted that call, we have the privilege to accept the call of Christ to become believers.

After my discharge, I caught a bus to my friend's home in New Jersey and stayed with his parents overnight. They provided a lovely breakfast the following morning. After breakfast, before they took me to the bus station, we had family devotions together. Family devotions, in a nut shell, is reading the Bible and praying for each other. That was the first time that I can remember anyone praying with and for me, other than my sister. Her promise to pray for my salvation in November 1950 was finally fulfilled around the same date in November 1952. God does answer prayer!

I arrived home on Christmas Eve just in time to enjoy my first Christmas as a Christian. On Sunday December 28, 1952 I went to the Wesleyan Church in Bradford, Pennsylvania for the first time. My parents and family never said, "We'll see how long this is going to last," but I had the feeling that it was in the back of their minds. They were well aware of my past performances, and truthfully, I would have asked the same question. The answer is that except in cases of sickness or real emergencies, I go every week. I have gone for sixty-two years and counting.

My problem was that I was adjusting not only to civilian life, but also to the Christian lifestyle. I was able to get a job early in January 1953 at Speer Resistor Corporation in Bradford, Pennsylvania as a quality control engineer. They asked about my discharge on my application, and I was hired in spite of that fact. My work consisted of checking the physical dimensions of resistors and coil forms as well as their electrical characteristics and performances. I had the evening shift and was on my own. I met a girl there who was the youth pastor at a Pentecostal Church. We went to our own churches on Sunday mornings, and on Sunday evenings we alternated between the two. The Wesleyan Church preached sanctification, while the Pentecostal Church preached on being baptized in the Spirit and speaking in tongues.

It did not take long before I questioned, "Lord, what do you want for me and what is right for me?" During my hour lunch break at Speer Resistor, I started to pray and fast about what God wanted for my life. It would be about a year before I had that answer. I prayed, "Lord, I want to know which one is right for me. Turn me every way but loose." Eventually he would do exactly that. Then, another problem surfaced. I began to feel the call of God to be a pastor. You need to remember, I had been divorced. I reminded the Lord, "I have drank and smoked. I have been divorced. I've been kicked out of the Navy." The list was long. God had other plans.

My pastor had scheduled evening missionary services at our church in May 1953. He used missionaries who were attending Houghton College in Houghton, New York. On May 16th, he scheduled a Baptist missionary from Cuba to speak. I do not know what he preached about. However, God's call to be a pastor was clearly on the plate. It was our custom that after a speaker had preached, the people would meet him in the aisles of the church to express their appreciation. As I shook his hand, and before I could open my mouth, he said this to me: "Mister, I have never seen such a sour-lemony pickled-faced puss in all my life. If I was you, I would do something about it." I immediately thought about what he said, and I went out on the porch of the Church. I stood watching the full moon. In my heart I said to myself, "If that is what it means to say 'No' to God, I am going to say 'Yes!'" I have never regretted that answer. God has been gracious to me!

Another problem had been solved, but another took its place. I needed a college education to even think about becoming a pastor. I had only finished the 11th grade, and that was nine years before. Shortly thereafter, the Registrar from Houghton College visited our church. She was the pastor's sister-in- law. He arranged an interview for me. She later wrote and told me that if I could take a General Educational Development test and pass every area with above a 45th-percentile rank, I could be admitted to the college on probation. I passed all five required tests. My lowest was percentile-rank was 62, and my highest was 92. One problem solved. Another takes it place. In the fall of 1953, I contacted the U.S. Veterans Administration, and through it and Houghton College, I was able to obtain funds that would permit my acceptance in the spring semester, on February 4, 1954. They offered me housing in the Old College Inn, and I was able to eat at the college dining hall. I was all set.

My daughter Sandra was a part of the equation. In 1953, I was renewing my responsibilities as her father. I asked my mother if she would continue to take care of her when I went to college and until I could make arrangements for her to live with me. My father and mother agreed. I want you to know that when I exited the Navy, my total worth was $139.26. Most of that was spent getting me home and taking care of needs until I found employment. I can affirm that God does provide! The above gives you insight into what God can do. More later!

New Beginnings

"Off with the old and on with the new" describes my life during 1953. It gives a glimpse of my intertwined life as a civilian and as a Christian, and all of the things that went on in my life. By the time I went to college, I had accepted my "Macedonian call." I had become engaged to Joanne, a youth pastor. That lasted until the end of the first semester. We decided separately that getting married was not God's will for our lives. We went and viewed a mutual friend, and when we exited the funeral home, she went one way and I went the other. We both knew that our choice was pleasing to God.

In my first semester, I took the required 15 semester hours. I had Principles of Writing 1 and 2 from two different instructors. While Professor Jo was teaching me sentence structure, Professor Lennox was teaching me punctuation or poetry. I was one messed up first semester student. They got their teaching methods together and each of them tutored me where I need help. Dr. Nelson was my psychology professor. He almost convinced me I needed professional counseling. Dr. Shea taught sociology and he thought his class was the only one that was important, so I learned to read. He had a different way of teaching. You only had to be present in his class. You might sleep, knit, or whatever and we did. He read the text that we were supposed to read with his glasses on, only removing them when he lectured briefly. His average on and off was 145 times during a class period. This is not figurative, nor is it an exaggeration; members of the class kept count. Somehow, he instilled in me a desire for social services work. Mrs. McMillen was my Introduction to Bible Professor. Through their hard work, I finished those courses with a 2.5 GPA. This ended my probationary period at the College. Dr. Robert Ferm, Dean of Men, had accepted responsibility for me during my stay at the college. I am sure he breathed a sigh of relief. I thank God for those that played such an important part in my life. Their contribution to my life and ministry for 62 years has been invaluable.

I was able to get work in the dining hall as a breakfast cook helper. My work consisted of helping to get the breakfast meal ready and breaking out cases of whatever was needed for lunch and dinner. A case of applesauce opened into a serving bowl and was placed in the cooler. It might be peas, beans or whatever else the cook would need for lunch or dinner that day. The last thing I had to do was dry the washed pans the cook had used that morning. It was a challenge, however it did help pay for my eating at the dining hall. I was young and it helped me then. Today, I am tired just thinking of the schedule.

By June 1956, I had met my academic requirements as a junior. This ended my College career. I had met Violet M. Marville on Memorial Day weekend in 1955. Violet's brother Robert asked me if I would go on a blind picnic on Memorial Day weekend in 1955, and I reluctantly consented. Violet had brought Robert's fiancée up to Houghton College to see him over the weekend, and he wanted someone to give him some freedom from his brotherly responsibilities. He had planned for a group of college friends to have a picnic at Letchworth State Park at the Wolfe Creek recreational area.

We stopped at all the sight-seeing events in the park. One was Inspiration Point where many a young couple has been inspired. There are three falls within the park: the Upper Falls, the Middle Falls and the Lower Falls. Each of them was picturesque in its own unique way. To this day, the Wolfe Creek area still holds a special place in my heart. Violet "Babe" and I had a ball. She had a 1954 yellow Chevrolet with green trim. We had mobility, but the best of all was wading and playing in Wolfe Creek that flowed through the area. In 1955 there were no "short shorts" or slacks-- proper girls dressed in dresses and silk hose even to picnics. Houghton College was a very conservative Christian College, and the picnic reflected that culture. One thing was sure: her panty hose were in shambles by the end of the day. Her friends could not believe that we had only just met.

Babe was a five foot two inch beauty with light brown hair and piercing black eyes. She was vivacious and had a fun-loving personality, which clicked with me. She worked at New Jersey Bell Telephone as an accounting clerk, and I was a full time student with part time jobs, raising my daughter, and at the same time preaching at churches on the weekends and holding evangelistic services. My friend, Robert Reagan^, did the booking for us and saw that some of the services took us to New Jersey. Violet and he were a part of the same youth ministry in the Wesleyan Church at Camden, New Jersey. At the same time, she found occasion to bring family and friends to see her brother Robert at Houghton. There were no cell phones back then, but the U. S. Postal Service kept us in constant communication.

There were several circumstances that happened that brought us together. The first of these was my birthday in October of 1955. I had been discharged from the U. S. Navy on December 22, 1952, I had worked during 1953, at Spear Resistor Corporation in Bradford, Pennsylvania, and I had started College, February 4, 1954, and my clothes were wearing out. I started praying about the fact that I needed clothes and shirts especially.

May I digress for a bit? "Mom"- Mrs. Betsy Ackers^ was a cook at Houghton College. She had taken my daughter, Sandra, and me under her wing. She would come to our apartment on her day off and make sure it was clean and help to get a decent meal on the table. One day, she gave me a package and had me open it. It contained two white shirts with French cuffs, cufflinks and tie clips as well. At this time, the Wesleyan Church was very strict. Some men did not wear ties or any jewelry. I can remember her saying to me, "I am tired of your ties flopping all over the place. Wear them!" She was a quiet, loving Saint of the Lord who was as sweet as she was firm. She was a great grandmother figure for my daughter and a great mentor in the Christian Faith for me. She was a kindly and beautiful Christian lady.

Violet, on the other hand, noticed that I needed some shirts. She bought me two for my birthday and sent them to me in the mail. They were corduroy. One of them was gray and the other was pink. I want you to know that in the 1950's, very few men wore bright colored shirts let alone pink ones. How was I going to wear the pink one? I went to prayer again. "Lord, I can't wear that one." Jesus and I have a working relationship, and in His own unique way he said, "You prayed and I have answered." That settled the question. If He did not mind a pink shirt, why should I? By the way, I still love the color pink.

Sometime in April 1956, Violet visited the campus once again. On Saturday morning, we met at the College dining Hall at 8:30 AM for breakfast. She was staying the weekend with her sister. After breakfast, we went to Sand Hill where there was a place you could talk and visit. I had been divorced, and the Church took a dim view of divorced people remarrying. She had no problem with it. That was not true for me. However, as we read from James 1:1-5 (KJV) these words popped out at me, **"But let patience have her perfect work, that ye may be perfect and entire wanting nothing. If any of you lack wisdom, let him ask God, that gives to all men liberally, and upbraids not; and it shall be given him."** That morning, even though what I read had nothing to do with marriage, it made sense as we were praying.

We determined to get married. After Violet returned home, she wrote me a letter and explained that she had had a radical mastectomy in 1952 and that her right breast was removed because of cancer. I wrote her and affirmed that that would not make any difference to me.

Between April and July 7th, there was a flurry of activity. She got her ring in New Jersey and I got mine at Houghton at the grocery store for $10.00. Today the ring would sell for about $250.00. Violet got everything going on her end, and I did the same on my end. The college year ended June 1st. My friend, Robert, provided me transportation to Gibbsboro, New Jersey. I managed to get my blood test done and to obtain the marriage license. There was one glitch. I had to take a bus from Camden to Olean, NY. When I arrived in Olean there was about five inches of snow on the ground. I hitched a ride to Houghton that was about 40 miles north. One thing I remember was that this was Commencement and they were holding it outside on the Commons. It warmed up to be a nice sunny warm day.

My one problem that I had to solve was who would marry us. Her pastors told her that she might use the church. However, because of the divorce they were not permitted to marry us. My friend Robert and I had travelled as Evangelists for about two years and had worked for the

Salvation Army many times. I asked Major Harold and Margery Spencer, his wife, if they would marry us. They were the Commandants in Wellsville, New York. They were very agreeable. It was hot day on July 7th -- about 100 degrees. During the wedding I almost passed out. A glass of water and a fan helped out a lot.

Later that evening, we left for our honeymoon. We stayed in Laurel, Maryland on our first night, and spent the following week viewing the sights of "Skyline Drive" in Virginia. It was in Maryland that my oldest son was conceived. The next morning, she informed me that her "monthly visitor" was a part of the picture. On Sunday, July 8th we had breakfast and she had Bible devotions prior to going to Church. This set the tone for our marriage. She read Psalm 27 and prayed before we went to the Southern Baptist Church in Laurel, Maryland. After lunch that day, we began our tour of "Skyline Drive". *"Skyline Drive is a National Scenic Byway that runs 105 miles north and south along the Blue Ridge Mountains in Shenandoah National Park. There are 75 overlooks that offer stunning views of the Shenandoah Valley to the west or the rolling piedmont to the east. Fall is an especially popular time to travel along Skyline Drive, with its colorful foliage from late September to mid-November,"* says the Google Tourist Map of Virginia.

Our marriage put an end to my college career. At that time, the college would not let a divorced person that had remarried matriculate. I had completed my major requirements for Comprehensive Christian Education with minors in Greek, Psychology and Sociology. The courses that I needed for ordination, I would take by correspondence to finish my college work. I did not graduate from high school, and I do not carry a degree from College. I did manage to earn four credit hours in a post-graduate course for Prison Chaplaincy in January 1979. I wrote a paper titled, "The Problems of the Homosexual In and Out of the Criminal Justice System." I got an A+ in that course. A requirement was that the article had to be published. It was published in the Summer Issue of July 1957, of *The Journal of the Association of Evangelical Institutional Chaplains.* I was subsequently endorsed as a Prison Chaplain.

My pastoral ministry began on June 13, 1954. I was asked to pastor the Lamont, New York Community Church. It was a school house church located about 25 miles from Houghton College. Other students helped with Sunday school, Vacation Bible School, and other programs. When I started as their pastor, we had about 20-25 people. I was forced by my academic work load at college to resign from the church. Our average had increased to about 35 in the year and a half that I had pastored the church.

In the fall of 1955, my daughter Sandra wanted us to be together. I got an apartment and I became a single parent. I told Sandra in April of 1956 that I was going to get married, and we would have to move to a house. By this time she did not like all the moving. I can hear her reply, "Change, change, change." She never did come to a place where she liked change in her life. Our address was 15 Smith Drive, Houghton NY 14744. We had telephone service on a 12 party line. Our backyard neighbor would intercept our calls if we were not available and immediately upon our availability, she would let us know who had called. You had to have patience when you wanted to use the telephone

I had made some lasting college friendships while at Houghton. There was Paul, Jim, Wayne and Brick, Don and Marty, Ruth, and Grace. It was great because when Sandra came to live with me, I suddenly needed babysitters on occasion. They graciously supplied my need for free. I could call and say, "Sandra is coming over," give them the time, and they made sure that she got there when she was supposed to be. I could not have continued without their help. Paul and Jim taught her how to play ball. The others permitted her to become a part of their family activities while they took care of her. It worked. I praise God, and I thank the Christian Community of which I was a part for helping raise my daughter and helping me to obtain the education I needed.

My divorce from Valerie and subsequent remarriage was still standing in the way of my ordination, but God had other plans. I was pastoring the Free Methodist Church in Olean, New York, and I was up for ordination. But, before I could be ordained, according to the by-laws and rules of the Church, I had to prove that Valerie had remarried before I had married the third time.

How would I do that? I could not go up to her and ask her, "When did you get married? When did you have your first child?" Early in June 1967, I was visiting my mother and she asked, "Did you hear that Valerie's oldest son was killed in a shooting mishap?" I had not. I wrote to the Bradford Era Newspaper, Bradford, Pennsylvania, and asked if they could send me the article relative to his death. They were kind enough to send me the paper. This gave me all the information that I needed to provide our Board of Bishops with the information they needed to approve me for ordination.

Tears of Thanksgiving have often coursed down my cheeks as I consider the goodness of God. Through the unspeakable tragedy of Valerie's son's death, God worked that I might enter the ministry and receive my Deacon's ordination at Annual Conference in July 1969 and my Elder's Ordination on August 2, 1972.

The summer that Violet and I married, we were asked to pastor the Marshall Community Church in Belfast New York. In July 1957, we were asked to pastor the Federated Church in Ischua, New York for a year (See Appendix 5). Life was moving at a fast clip, and on April 16 of that same year, William T. Lowery, Jr. was born.

My oldest daughter, Sandra Elaine, was 11 years of age when we married. Bill Jr., our son, was born just nine months and nine days after our marriage. Two of my friends, Paul and James, prayed hard that there would be no doubt about the circumstances of his birth when they heard that he might be born two weeks early. They were friends that had your back and were concerned. Our second son, David Paul, waited two and a half years for his arrival, and Rebekah Sue was born six years and one day after her oldest brother. They were joined by Stephan Sharpe ^, a self-adopted son.

My namesake is Bill, Jr., and when he was born over 11 years after his sister, I had problems. He was born April 16, 1957. During my wife's pregnancy, I was a nervous wreck. The attending doctor finally told me, "Reverend, you take care of prayer and I'll take care of my patient." However, during my wife's 40 and a half hour labor, I was a basket case. The doctor had to give me medication to get me through it. It is a joy to look back on your life and note the differences in your children and the joy that those differences make. As he was being born the Lord gave me **Psalm 27:13-14** as a promise.

Early on, Bill, Jr. became the favorite of his mother. She protected him from his mean old father. I learned early on that when it came to disciplining him, we could not tell him "No!" or "Do this!" The best way was to give him about three choices, and he would normally pick out the way to go.

I enjoyed watching him grow into manhood. He played football as number 70. I was never good at any sport and I am not to this day. He got his first job working in a True Value store and would eventually buy his first car. He decided that God wanted him to be a minister and told a mentor of his that he had accepted God's call on his life. He never told me, however. The mentor happened to tell me about six months after the fact. I had a rough time as he went to college. I could no longer look out for him. Now that we are both older and he feels free to let the cat out of the bag, I'm learning that I had every reason to be concerned. However, I can now laugh at some of his antics.

His brother, David Paul, was born October 17, 1959 at about 11:30 PM. There is a vast difference between the two boys. Bill, Jr. takes after his maternal grandfather in many of the ways he walks and does things. David, on the other hand, takes after his paternal grandfather. You would know they were related if you would ever saw them together. David had an attitude about him and still does that is like his grandfather's. You could tell him to behave, and all the time you were telling him, he would be telling you why he should continue doing what he was doing and he would continue to do it. I still watch him and try to change him, but it does not do any good. God gave me **Psalm 100:4-5** while he was being born. There are times when my children are going through rough times that I remind God of their particular verse.

When my boys got into their mid-teens, I told them that the manner of discipline in our house was no more paddling, but to get clobbered on the end of the chin. One day, David tried it out. I was ticked by whatever he was doing, and I invited him outside. I purposed to go out first. Wham! He would get it as came out the door. He graciously opened the door for the "Old man," and as I stepped out, he slammed it shut, set the lock, and stood in the door laughing at me. I didn't clobber him, and now I chuckle as I realize that he knew how to handle me. I was ticked. He was having fun with the "Ole Man," his affectionate name for me.

David followed his brother, only he got a job as a plumber's helper. He still follows the trade to this day, though he is now an air conditioning and heating specialist. He got a Jeep as his first car, and I helped him to put a particle board top on it. It was my job to keep it going. He played football as number 64, and he wrestled like his big brother. He would follow him to college and earn a degree in History and Religion. He currently works on a Christian College Campus as an Air Conditioning and Heating (AV/HT) mechanic. When he got married, I gave the job of keeping his Jeep running to his new father-in-law. Over the years, I have heard about my sneaky trick and have had a good chuckle as I accept the blame.

Life was fun at our house during our 23 years of marriage. We, in a sense, were raising a blended family, and this was under the scrutiny of the community and the Church. You can never be sure what is going to happen in a Pastor's parsonage. Babe (Violet) had grown up with seven brothers and sisters. She was the middle child and the one that was a catalyst for the others in her family. It was fun for "In-laws" or as we called ourselves "Out-laws." In her home, during family occasions, about 35 people would all be talking at the same time at the dinner table and they were keeping track of all the conversations at the same time. I mean it-- they talked full throttle!

People would be surprised if they knew that in 1962, I was an insurance salesman for John Hancock. I could sell insurance, as long as I did not mention Jesus or the Church. Every time I or someone else mentioned Jesus or the Church, I automatically quit selling insurance. Early in September, I was hospitalized with a severe kidney infection and was unable to make my quota of commissions. As I did not have enough time in sales, my commissions would not support me. I did not receive my "Training Allowance Pay" (TAP). I was out of a job.

By the time I found a job washing cars and changing tires for $1.25 an hour in December, we were eating potato soup on a regular basis. Some of my family still do not like potato soup to this day. That year, we received $65.00 for Christmas from friends and family. A day or two before Christmas, our pastor from the Church where we attended came to the house with a chicken (uncooked), some vegetables, and an apple pie. This gave us some time and money to prepare and to provide Christmas gifts for all three children. How grateful my wife Violet and I were for a church that cared and for a God that loved us.

I will never forget the joy we experienced as we celebrated the birth of our Savior Jesus Christ on the Christmas of 1962. I have had many other Christmases that were plusher, but none that made my worship of Jesus more meaningful. On April 17th 1963, our daughter Rebekah was born – a belated gift from God. I remember and praise and worship from my heart.

You talk about problems. My daughter, Rebekah Sue, was my fault. Her mother did not want to be pregnant, and for the nine months that she carried her, I felt I might be getting a divorce anytime. It was my fault. She was born April 17, 1963, at 6:30 PM. Her mother had sent me home to take care of the pets, and I arrived at the hospital waiting room just in time to hear the doctor say, "It's a girl." The problem was that she was supposed to be a boy. Since I was to name the girls, I did an admirable job of choosing her name. The verse that God gave me for her was **Jeremiah 15:16.**

Her mother told me early on that she was going to be a Little Miss Prim. However, when she came into her early teens, she could climb a tree and skin a cat with the best of the tomboys. It is amazing to realize that she took after her mother in a lot of ways. Her mother passed away from cancer when Rebekah was just sixteen years old. That fall, her brothers had both gone off to college. It was just her and me, and she was a handful at times. In the meantime, I had changed churches and pastorates. I just shudder to this day of thinking about the adjustments that happened to come our way. She decided to go to college to become a medical secretary. Everything was in place. However, she got married that fall. The best laid plans of mice and men... Her marriage was rocky for the first seven years. They divorced, but she and her husband finally got back together and today they are the Pastor and wife of a nice church. The amazing thing is that during this time she started working in a doctor's office and became a medical secretary. She currently works at a physical therapy office in that capacity.

Becky was an easy child to discipline. Only once do I remember having to dust her bottom. I only gave her one whack. However, one day when she was about seven, her mother called me at work. She had seriously threatened her mother that she was going to run away. Finally, Violet told her to wait until she got me on the phone. Violet told me what was happening. I ask that she be put on the phone. I simply told her, that she could not run away, and that I would not allow her to run away. She did not run away. But, if it is mentioned today when she is many years older, she still gets upset that she could not run away even though I was at work when I told her that. I still have a chuckle when I think of it. All I have to do is to mention it and let the fun begin.

Kids will be kids. When she was about 15, the three of them, Rebekah, Bill, and David were sitting and talking in the living room when they made a startling discovery. This was about a year before their mother's death. They had decided that Bill was Mom's favorite, David was Dad's favorite, and Becky had us both wrapped around her little finger. Finally, the truth was out, and how true it was.

The fifth child is a foster son of sorts. Stephen Sharpe^ adopted us. He was born July 31, 1954. His father had left the family when he was seven. Later in his life, he did reconnect with his father and was able to establish a relationship, but not a substantive one. He was invited to stay overnight at the beginning, and our boys would go to his house. Eventually, he would come and go whenever he felt the need. When he got in trouble at home, he would come to our house, and when he got in trouble at our house, he would go home. He would go home especially if

Maria^, my niece, was there and her boyfriend happened to show up. It was great to watch him grow up as part of our home and church family.

When we moved to another church about 60 miles away, he went with us. I have prayed for him for most of his life, and it has paid off. He is a Christian and works in Arizona, helping to operate a Christian Camp. There were times when we had to exercise parental discipline. There was the time that my wife was cleaning and found a couple of bottles of wine that he had tucked away. Our home always has been drink and smoke-free. The wine went down the drain, and he was told by Violet that he was never to bring wine into the house again. His birth mother appreciated the time that he spent with us, since he had two older brothers and a younger brother. He always maintained a close relationship with her, as well as with his self-adopted parents. I thank the Lord that I can call him my son.

Violet brought to our family what I didn't. She loved baseball, football, bowling, roller skating, and all kinds of sports. I can bowl well, but not too well. I can roller-skate acceptably well. Riding a bicycle I can manage to stay afloat most of the time. Let's not overdo it, now! Two incidents will help you to envision our family. But first I want you to envision her for a moment.

She was a proper parsonage queen. She always wore a pill box hat that matched her a-line dress with white gloves and shoes from Memorial Day to Labor Day. In the winter it was with black accessories. Babe would never permit you to say, "Shut up". You must always say "Be quiet," and she enforced her rule. She always baked bread, cookies, and more on Saturdays. One Saturday, she and our three children were making chocolate chip cookies, and things were not going too well. After about three times of asking them to be quiet, finally she had had it. She said very emphatically, "I said shut up!" Do you know what? It instantly had the effect that she desired. (I'm chuckling even as I write.)

The next one is that normally you had to have perfect manners at the table, if that is possible. But, once in a while, she would play table-tennis before you were excused. She would take her napkin, rolled tightly into a ball; and, you never knew who would receive her tennis-ball napkin in your tennis-glass of milk, or your tennis-cup of coffee. She was a dead shot. We soon caught up! There was one last rule at our house. You never had to say "Please" or "Thank you" after Church on Sunday evening. That was the time we relaxed and enjoyed both food and having a great time with family and friends. Good manners went out the window for the occasion! Life was fun.

Losing Violet

The prophet Isaiah writes concerning Jesus, **"He is despised and rejected by men, a Man of sorrows and acquainted with grief."** (Isaiah 53:3) I have struggled in my efforts to write about Violet's death. I immediately wanted to title this section **"Death and Dying."** It is about Violet's death and dying, but it encompasses so much more than that. It is about me. As I have thought about it, my three wives all died at the same time in the evening. On August 30th 1946, Marian Bradt died after delivery of our daughter, Sandra, at 8:15 P.M.; on May 8th at 8:15 P.M., Violet Marville died from a long battle with cancer; and on April 18th 2005 at 8:15.P.M, June Taylor-Lowery passed away after suffering a broken left femur and several complications. When I realized this it amazed me.

Before I met Violet, she had a radical mastectomy of her right breast. She had all of her breast removed including lymph nodes and part of the muscles to her right arm. They left nothing to chance. Later, as she ironed clothes, she would use her left hand to guide and help her right hand to iron, and the clothes were free of iron wrinkles. Violet fought ovarian cancer from 1976 to 1979. Though no doctor has told me this, I believe that her last bout began in 1975. In April of that year, she had a very bad case of bronchitis. She coughed the entire month, and, again, the same thing happened in October, causing problems through the middle of December. It came time to visit her family over the Christmas holiday, and we were afraid that she would not be able to make it, but as we were getting close to the deadline, she appeared alright.

We arrived safely in Gibbsboro, New Jersey, and immediately she began to have problems. She presumably was fighting a kidney infection. She drank cranberry juice, and it appeared to help. After we returned home, she seemed to get better. One evening, as we were getting ready for bed, I was playing mousey across her stomach. I felt what appeared to be a growth about the size of a large grapefruit. The next day we went to see her gynecologist, and they admitted her to the hospital. She had a hysterectomy and they removed everything including a very large tumor. After ten days in the hospital, they sent her to a large cancer hospital and they found another tumor up behind her stomach. In December of 1976, she had to have a section of her colon removed because of a blockage. This was followed by three years in and out of the cancer hospital. Blood tests were given for her platelet count and she went back into the hospital for blood transfusions and more chemotherapy. She went into remission during July and August of 1978, and when she went back for her checkup in September of that year, the cancer had returned. It was downhill from that point forward. After her death, three of her sisters suffered from ovarian and pancreatic cancer and succumbed because of their cancers.

It was later found out through medical history that our daughter, Rebekah, had some of the same symptoms that her mother had shown. They gave her a blood test that showed she had the BRCA2 gene that was associated with breast and ovarian cancer. Her Doctor advised her to have a hysterectomy, and she had the surgery. Later, they would find a lump in her breast and she would have a double mastectomy and reconstructive surgery on her breasts. She is cancer free. However, they keep close tabs on her. Later it has been found out that at least two of her cousins have the same BRCA2 gene. My un-medical advice to any woman that has either breast or ovarian cancer is to make sure you have regular checkups and share your complete history with your gynecologist.

A Letter to Myke

Dear Myke,

I am not suggesting that you have four wives or any wives. I would like you to think with me. I am so glad that I have never had to contend with "Four Wives" simultaneously. I think back to the Book of Genesis and remember Jacob. You may read the story of his life in Genesis 25: - 38: Please note that in this one verse, God is speaking, **"I am the God of Bethel, where you anointed the pillar and where you made a vow to me. Now arise get out of this land, and return to the land of your family.' (Genesis 31:13 NKJV)** I am sure you will want to read about your Grandmother June (Mia). First, may I recount a little of Jacob's history?

Isaac was 40 years old when his mother Sarah died. His father did not want him to take a daughter of the Canaanites, nor did he want him to return to Haran and select his own wife. Abram sent his servant to Haran to get a wife from his father's house-hold for his son, Isaac. The servant chose Rebekah. He made the arrangements with Laban, and Rebekah was willing to go and marry Isaac. They had no children for 20 years, until Isaac prayed to the Lord and Rebekah conceived. She learned that she was going to have twins. Esau and Jacob caused problems even before they were born, and at their birth Esau was born and as Isaac was born he grabbed his brother's heel. It turned out that Isaac preferred Esau and Rebekah preferred Jacob. Jacob means "a conniver". One day as Esau was coming from the field and was "starving," he sold his birthright to Isaac for a bowl of lentils (vegetable soup).

Later, nearly-blind Isaac sent Esau to go hunting and to make him a savory stew which Isaac liked and he would bless him. But, Rebekah heard the plans. She sent Jacob to get two kid goats and she made savory stew. She covered Jacob's hands and neck with the goat skins so that Isaac would not recognize him. She dressed Jacob in his brother's clothes, in order that even his smell would fool Isaac. Isaac received his father's blessing just prior to Esau coming in to feast his Father and obtain the blessing. Needless to say, Esau was not too happy. He planned Jacob's death. Before he could complete his plan, Rebekah had Isaac send Jacob to get a wife in Haran where his Uncle Laban lived. He spent the first night at Bethel. In the morning he took the rock that he had used as a pillow and anointed it with oil and he promised God that if He made his way successful that he would worship Him upon his return.

Jacob met his match in Uncle Laban. Jacob promised to work for Rachael, who he desired as his wife, for seven years. On his wedding night, Uncle Laban substituted Leah, Rachel's older sister, for the bride. He was surprised in the morning. However, his uncle Laban allowed him to marry Rachel a week later for another seven years work. The two connivers would continue their bargaining until Jacob owned most of his uncles' cattle, sheep, etc. Twenty years passed and God sent Jacob home. Thus, we have the highlighted portion above. However, Jacob will have to deal with his brother Esau. Remember, God said, **"I am the God of Bethel."**

It comes time to write about your Mia.

Yours in Love,

Dad

Completing Our Family

Myke, you probably do not remember. However, it began August 17, 1980. It was the first time Mia and her family visited our Church. That undoubtedly included her, your mother (Pat), your brother Matthew, your sister Minta, and you. That was the Sunday that I had a VISA missionary to Japan speak for me. He had been in Japan for at least two years and had married a Japanese woman. I cannot remember his or her name. The thing that I do remember was that he preached for well over an hour. I am sure that all the ladies of the Church could think of was burnt chicken or over done roast. Your Mia told me later that only one person, Bette^, spoke to her, and that June had her children in school. Mia told me that she decided that she was not coming back to that unfriendly church. To those reading this, June was Myke's Grandmother. His father called her Mama Mia. Myke shortened the name to Mia. The name stuck, not only for the grandchildren; "Mia" became the favorite for both family and friends.

Near the first of October of that year, Rebekah came to me and expressed her concern for me. I was alone most of the time. Becky was a very active teenager, and she was very concerned that I was home alone often when my duties as a Pastor were completed. She said, "Dad, you cannot just sit around and do nothing." I told her then, "Becky, the only way that I am going to go out with anyone is for God to bring someone in the back door and say, 'This is it.'" However, this did get me to thinking. For my birthday, October 25th, I went down to the Poconos to see Violet's sister and brother-in- law, and then on to Lititz, Pennsylvania to see my daughter Sandra. As I left the Poconos, I travelled down I-81 South and I was praying. I came to myself going over 85 miles an hour or more and crying my eyes out. I had the sense to pull over to the side of the road at a road marker that read "Bethel." In Hebrew that township marker means, "House of God." I came home and thought no more about it. Bethel undoubtedly meant the township into which I was entering.

God was working with Mia. She had decided to go to a Pentecostal Church in the village, and she did. But, on January 4th 1981, God impressed upon her that He wanted her to go back to the Free Methodist Church. She argued with God, but she lost that one. She noted, "The people were a lot friendlier than they were in August." On January 18th, I had heard that she was worshipping with us. At the end of the service, as I was dismissing the congregation following the worship service, a lovely redhead shook my hand and winked at me. She told me later, "I did not." I want the world to know that I know a wink when I see one, especially from a beautiful woman.

The Lord was working in other ways during the month of January. The children's and youth ministries were off the charts. I had no place for the midweek prayer except the Sanctuary or the parsonage, which was across the drive. We decided to use the parsonage. My friend Ray helped me set up chairs for the change. After the prayer meeting was over, as he was taking the chairs out of the house and back to the church, he made this statement: "Mister, she came tip-toeing in the back door. She did not like the way I put the chairs and changed them all around, and you are just plain sunk." Myke, I made all the necessary calls as any good Pastor should. She invited Rebekah and me to your house for dinner. I do not remember the menu, but I am sure of this: it was delicious.

Our relationship became serious. On March 17th, 1981, I was at the Bishop's School of Renewal. I do not know which Bishop it was, but he was Dullsville on this occasion. Every time I tried to listen, all that I could see was a redhead. Subsequently, I asked a pastor friend if I could use his phone. He took me into his office, and I popped the question. She said, "Yes, but we have some issues to iron out." It was then that she shared with me that she was the guardian of Michael Patrick, her grandson, whose birth mother is Pat. Pat's first husband had left and divorced her for a male friend, even before there were same-sex marriages. She had three children to provide for, and it was too much for her to accomplish on her own. Her children were Michael, Matthew and Minta. June had taken Myke under her wing and helped with the other children as well. She let me know that she was his guardian and she asked "If that was alright with me." Naturally, I said, "Yes." She set the date for 140 days hence for August 1, 1981. I counted every one of them. That is a long time.

I want to assure you that I had told June about the United States Navy and my orientation even before asking her to marry me on March 17, 1981. I want to affirm that I have maintained my integrity and faithfulness to Mia to this day. Never once did I ever want to hurt her or my new family members.

We no sooner announced our engagement when the ladies of the church approached her and asked for her to have me put plastic liners in the garbage cans. They had never had a single pastor prior to this, and used her to get things ship shape. We married as planned. We honeymooned in Toronto, Canada. August 3rd was a little rough. It was the Canadian National Holiday. We both came down with a stomach bug. On the 4th we happened to get a small suite in a motel that was reserved for the owner of the motel. It was perfect for our Honeymoon. When we got home we had to get her household furniture in with mine. We managed the seemingly impossible. I am sure that Myke realized that there was rough going sometimes.

Sherry Lee Taylor was born on January 25, 1952. She did not become a part of the Taylor family until about 1959. She had been abandoned by her mother and given to an elderly couple who took care of her until she was seven years old. Rev. Wallace and June (Mia) had been asked to be guardians of her, and they finally adopted her. I have no knowledge of the details of her adoption other than these.

Sherry's father died on January 27, 1980, and I married her mother on August 1, 1981. She had a hard time after her father's death, and she wanted to know who she was. On the back of her birth certificate, someone had written her mother's and father's names in pencil. Her mother was Grace Field^, and her father was Adam Gustafson^. She also knew that she was born in Lewisburg, PA. I told her that after Easter on April 11, 1982, when I had my vacation, that I would take her down and see what we could find out. We went to Lewisburg and obtained motel accommodations. When we went to the hospital in Lewisburg, the one thing we did find out was that she did have other brothers and sisters, but they could tell us nothing more. The hospital was not allowed to give out that information, and they told us that the only way we could get that information was if the courts declared that she had a medical emergency.

That evening, we looked in the telephone directory. Under her mother's name there were pages of Fields. We looked under her father's name and we hit pay dirt. Mrs. Gustafson told us we might visit the home in Milton, Pennsylvania the next morning at 10:00 AM. We entered the home and gave her the information that we had. Her father drove eighteen-wheelers and was not at home. As we entered the home, there was a life-size picture of his niece on the wall. I must say that it was a near image of Sherry, even to the clothes they were wearing. They had no information as to her mother Grace. Later, her father would try to find her, but to no avail. Sherry was able to make contact with her father. Sherry and her husband made friends with her father and his wife. They would eventually go camping and fishing together, which both families loved. Sherry finally had roots that made her feel that she belonged. The amazing thing is that she calls me dad, and that I am proud to call her my daughter.

I later learned that Mrs. Gustafson had heart problems. I still get chills when I think about what might have happened. The shock of being confronted over the phone the night before and the shock of having someone walk in that looked like her recently deceased niece may have caused a heart attack. I thank the Lord that oftentimes He takes care of us in our blunderings. We learned from her Father that around the time that Sherry was born, there were three couples who motorcycled together. They paired up with whoever was available. They knew that Grace was pregnant. However, she never revealed who the father was. Her father later told Sherry that if he had known about the situation, he would have taken care of her and her mother. I thank God that once in a while you stumble into situations and God sees you through.

On July 11, 1982, we were invited to a luncheon at the United Methodist Church. As we were finishing our dessert, Myke said, "Dad, I do not feel as though I belong to anyone." Mia and I had guardianship of him, which was a little rough at times. I purposed then and there that we would rectify that. We contacted his mother, Pat, and our lawyer, and proceeded with the adoption. We could not find his father. The court received nothing from him. They declared that we could adopt Myke with the consent of your mother. One thing that they needed was a background check on me. I will never forget the day I had to tell Myke that I might not be able to adopt him because of my orientation and my "Other Than Honorable Discharge" from the Navy. Praise the Lord, I passed muster. The adoption was completed on January 27th, 1983, and Myke you became our son. Our first meal celebrating the fact was a little rough. You were not too pleased with the hamburgers in Avon. Then, it was a rough bump in the road. Now, I look back and smile because of the memory with a twinkle in my eye.

The heat of the conflict continued until Myke went to college in September of 1987. There were near knock down and drag out conflicts during the six year period. Prior to our marriage June had mentioned to me several times that Myke need a good male mentor. As I observed his lifestyle, I questioned everything: the way he dressed and the way he acted caused me to believe that he was gay. Her response was, "Just because he dresses differently does not mean that he is gay." There were at least two occasions when I went personally and received counseling because of the relationship within the family. I tried to have him go with me, but Myke would not go along with family counseling. I came to the point at one time where I was seriously thinking of suicide. I was looking out the window in the breakfast nook in the parsonage about four in the evening. I had considered several ways to get the task done. However, I was afraid that I would not complete the job successfully and I did not want them or other members of my family to be hurt.

I knew that if I took one step away from the window that afternoon, I would accomplish what I purposed, no matter whether I succeeded or not. I went for counseling, for which I thank God. One other time I had thoughts of suicide. I had had a stroke and the thoughts were there. On this occasion, June called the family together and she made sure that all of the guns were removed from our home. I recovered and am thankful that she had the foresight to protect me.

It was hard to establish rapport in our home. June and Myke would sit at one end of the table and talk very softly, leaving me out in the cold. I talked with a voice that could be heard very well in a sanctuary, with or without a microphone. This even extended to discipline within the home. His Mom was a schoolteacher. When she left for work, Myke and I would invariably get into a hassle over something. She came home around 5 PM each evening, and we would get the problem worked out, but when she went to work the next day, we had problems again.

He and I even hassled over his contact lenses. He was in the kitchen and was able to put one in his eye, but something happened and he lost the other one. Needless to say, he did not wear contacts that day. After he left for school, I looked for it on the floor. I finally found it about 15 feet away, on the buffet in the dining room. I do not know how it got there to this day, but I know that it happened. The years have passed, and we understand each other better and have a fine relationship. The one hindrance is that we live about 100 miles apart.

Myke went to college in September 1987, in Rochester, New York. I questioned him several times about college and what was happening, and he told me on one occasion that he was on Monroe Avenue shopping. I was not aware of the Rochester area as well as I am today. At the time, Monroe Avenue was a very real part of the gay community. On November 15, 1987, just prior to going back to college, Myke came out to his mother and me. Even though I suspected the fact, both of us were devastated. I cancelled the 6:00 P.M. service. We prayed and cried. Yes, there are high points in ministry, but there are also low points. Since he was actively involved in the LGBT Community, he was not permitted to return to college for the spring semester. He got a job in Marketplace Mall in Rochester, New York selling cookies. He lived at our home with a friend until he was able to get an apartment in the city.

The summer of 1988 was an experience. My daughter Rebekah asked to come home. Her two sons were there too, especially on weekends. June's daughter, Pat, and her two children came to live with us after the split up of her marriage. A friend that had been in jail needed a home and help in being rehabilitated. There were eleven or twelve that were living in our home during that summer. Things were hectic to say the least.

The next two of my children are stepchildren. Patricia Ann Taylor Lyke is the daughter of June, my fourth wife. She was born on January 4, 1949, the daughter of Rev. Wallace and June Taylor. Her parents were missionaries to Kentucky for seven years where he pastored and where she taught school. They moved back to central New York and pastored several churches. He passed away on January 27, 1980. In the last several years, Pat proudly points to the fact that I have been her father longer than her real father, and I am happy to claim that distinction.

Only once have I ever had a run-in with her. She tried to rearrange my garage and she learned that it is a no-no. It has been my privilege to help raise my two grandchildren, Matt and Minta. It is almost like having two extended people to whom you can be a father. It is great to be used by God to help establish people in the Faith. Pat is the mother of my adopted son, Myke, to whom I have dedicated my biography. He was part of the package deal when I married his grandmother, Mia.

Pat lived with us during the summer of 1988. Her second marriage had fallen apart and she needed a place to stay. She finally found one, and I got help to move her from our home to an apartment. Ralph Lyke was a widower, and he helped her move not once, but twice. He moved her into an apartment, and they started to go together. When he finally married her, he moved her to their home. Ralph was a friend and also one of my parishioners. He and Pat made a wonderful couple. He passed away following heart surgery in 2009.

As my first daughter, Sandra, grew up, she continued to be an incredible blessing and a wonderful reminder of my first marriage. She followed in her mother's footsteps and became a nurse. She worked hard for her Registered Nurse's degree, and she graduated at the bottom of her class with the honor of being the most improved student, a distinction for which she received a certificate and a $250.00

award. As far as I know, she never nursed as a floor nurse. She always ended up being the supervising nurse on the floor in the hospital. She became so proficient at chemotherapy that she headed the unit in her hospital and at one time went to Japan and Singapore to teach chemotherapy with a medical team. She finished her career in nursing as a coding nurse for the hospital. She checked up on everyone else to see if they were performing their nursing duties in the right way.

As I think of all my children, blessings from God, a hymn of the Church comes to my mind entitled "My Savior's Love." I desire to pick out about four lines for your thought:

"I stand amazed in the presence Of Jesus the Nazarene ...

He took my sins and my sorrows; He made them his very own ...

How marvelous How wonderful! And my song shall ever be ...

How marvelous, how wonderful is my Savior's love for me? "

By Charles H. Gabriel

"I stand amazed" when I consider eight children and realize "How wonderful is my Savior's love for me." I have been the patriarch of my family for fifty years. As near as I can roughly figure, I have over 400 children, grandchildren, great-grandchildren, and great-great-grandchildren, and that figure includes, as well, many, many, nieces and nephews. I am blessed and "I stand amazed." I praise God as I sing, "How marvelous, how wonderful is my Savior's love for me? Amen!"

Problems and problem solving are a part of marriages. One of those problems was trying to blend our families together too soon after our marriage. The Lowery children had set Memorial Day Weekend for their time of family reunion. They had been meeting for about three years when June and I married. I had come to our marriage with all kinds of family relationships. A stepfather, step-uncles, a foster brother, family with family friendships, a foster-son, nieces and nephews from previous marriages-- they had all been a part of my life. My theory was to just keep them coming and that everything would work out. However, that did not work in this case. On Memorial Day weekend in 1982, my kids objected to my including my new family members into their reunion. They have worked out the kinks so to speak, but I am not sure that everything is completely as it might be.

Another problem that surfaced for me was that I felt like I was always out in left-field. It took awhile for June, Myke, and I to work out the fact that they were playing in the in-field and that I felt as though I was away out in left-field. At least, that is my point of view. As I said before, June (Mia) and Myke conversed in a very quiet manner, while I was much more boisterous. If there was a problem, I made sure that my point of view prevailed. After the incident was taken care of, if you did not like what I did, then we would talk. In my family, you changed the rules after everything became calm again. I wish I could do it over! I am sure that I would do things differently. This type of autocratic discipline led to many a confrontation. I am sure they wondered at times, "Why doesn't he just go somewhere else?" I will welcome my son Michael's, as well as the rest of the family's responses to my observation.

One other problem surfaced, and it was mine. When I married June, I loved her, but it was not the same. I got to thinking, "If I had to make a choice, which one of the three would I choose to live with?" I had been married four times. The second marriage ended in divorce. That one was out. My first marriage was love at first sight and all that goes with your first love. My third marriage was raising a family. When my oldest son was born, that Tuesday morning as I drove to work I was ten feet tall and no one had ever done it before, as far as I was concerned. I remembered Jacob having four wives all at once, according to the Bible. When June and I married, we decided that she would be buried by her former husband, and I would get buried with my children's mother. That way, our children would have their mothers and fathers all in one place when they visited their graves. Who would I choose? The Lord took a hand in this matter. He does involve himself in the affairs of men!

At our devotional time with the Lord at breakfast on September 28, 2002, **Matthew 6:21** and Our Daily Bread selection for the day was **(Ezekiel 24:15-24).** They were given to me by the Lord concerning my wife, June. Essentially, God admonished me twice that morning, to "LOVE YOUR WIFE." He did it as I read the promise verse and prayed before breakfast and, the second time as I was reading the Ezekiel passage. Yes, I loved her! On this occasion, God was instructing me to take care of her especially. Little did I know that on October 2nd, just four days away that she was going to have another angina heart attack? I obeyed God until the day He took her to be with Him on April 18, 2006. I do not remember if I ever told her. This one thing I do know: it paid off. We experienced a greater love for each other during that time for which "I thank the Lord."

June fell and broke her leg on March 17, 2005. It never healed correctly. Other medical complications became a part of the picture. She had three operations during this time, and she suffered a bleed in the brain during her sickness. I got to thinking, "I would like to get buried with her," when I saw the inevitable coming. I brushed it off. One day in November she asked me, "Can we get buried together?" I wisely said, "We will need to talk about this." Subsequently, when her two daughters were home for Christmas I questioned them. They had no problems. The decision was made in the affirmative that we would be buried together. I had a dilemma, "Who would I pick?" To be safe, I plead the fifth. I know one thing: my Wonderful Savior taught me how to love my beloved wife, June.

I decided when June passed away, that that was enough for me. I have not dated anyone since her death. I am not ruling out that God may have other ideas. I will deal with that whenever it might happen.

The God of the universe is in a battle to the death with Satan. Sometimes that battle is waged in our personal lives. It was waged in Paul's life. He talks about his sufferings in 2 Corinthians 11:16-29. (NKJV) He says in part referring to false prophets, in verses 22-25; **"Are they Hebrews? So am I. Are they Israelites? So am I. Are they the seed of Abraham? So am I. Are they ministers of Christ?—I speak as a fool— I am more: in labors more abundant, in stripes above measure, in prisons more frequently, in deaths often. From the Jews five times I received forty stripes minus one. Three times I was beaten with rods; once I was stoned; three times I was shipwrecked; a night and a day I have been in the deep."**

The above devotional time reference was taken from my personal Eagle Flight Diary, as well as the following verse. **"But those who wait on the Lord shall renew their strength; they shall mount up with wings like EAGLES, they shall run and not be weary, they shall walk and not faint." (Isaiah 40:31 NKJV)** God is Faithful. Amen!

PART FOUR: CORRECTIONAL CHAPLAINCY

Luke 4:16-19 New King James Version (NKJV)

"So He came to Nazareth, where He had been brought up. And as His custom was, He went into the synagogue on the Sabbath day, and stood up to read. And He was handed the book of the prophet Isaiah. And when He had opened the book, He found the place where it was written:

'The Spirit of the Lord is upon Me,
Because He has anointed Me
To preach the gospel to the poor;
He has sent Me to heal the brokenhearted,
To proclaim liberty to the captives
And recovery of sight to the blind,
To set at liberty those who are oppressed;
To proclaim the acceptable year of the Lord.'"

I left out a very important part of my ministry of 32 years. I did not realize how this would affect one of my special friends. As I talked with him this past week, I could tell the keen disappointment that he felt. Later, I was perusing some of my mementos of ministry and I realized that I had left out a part of my life that needed to be included. I knew that it was important and at the same time not the same, since I could not use real names. I loved this part of my ministry and many of the men that were a part of it. However, I have received permission to include this ministry in my autobiography as long as I use all pseudonyms. I have done so.

A Letter to Myke

Dear Myke,

I do not know if you have ever been in a jail or not. Sometimes in school they have you go on field trips. I know that your brother David had to go on one once, and I am sure that he would not go on his own volition ever again.

One thing is this: you never forget the first time you are put into a cell and the key snaps the lock shut. I can still hear how it sounded early in July of 1952. My cell number was B-2-1. The "B" was for B-blocks. The two was for six cells in one block, and I had the privilege of occupying the first cell of six. I do not remember who occupied the others. There were at least six blocks, and number four block housed people that needed what they called the "Black Box". I am glad that I never had to visit that particular block. That was the same cell that I occupied on two occasions. I would return to it on November 4th of 1952. The best I can remember was that I spent 69 days in the United States Naval Brig at Boston, Massachusetts. However, there are times when God turns things upside down. The Navy was interested in getting me out of the service because of my lifestyle. Twenty-two years later, God would send me back to jail as part of my ministry at the Free Methodist Church in Perry, New York. This would be the beginning of 29 years of going to jail, and after that, going back for three years of Bible Study with inmates every Thursday in 2010 through 2012.

When, I first went to the Wyoming County Jail, it was to visit with inmates and tutor them in preparation for taking their General Educational Development (GED) tests. This enabled them to receive their diplomas so that they could graduate from high school. As, part of the tutoring I would give them their pre-test and certify them to be able to take the GED test. Then, the person who was certified as the Chief Examining Officer by New York State for Wyoming County Jail would give the test. I began my ministry in the Old Jail, and I would continue there until December 1991. The old jail sat where the current Court

House is situated. It was originally the Sheriff's House and it had cells in which to house inmates. The Sheriff and the necessary offices were on the first floor, and upstairs was the Sergeants' Office. There were four or five beds for juvenile inmates behind the office. Juveniles were inmates who had not reached their seventeenth birthdays. Also, on the second floor was Two North, which had six cells for adults. There were about three cells for women. All told, we could house about twenty-five inmates.

The Department of Corrections (DOC) would mandate that Wyoming County would build a new facility. It got to the point where we did not have enough cells to care for the inmate population in Wyoming County. They purchased at least one house and tore it down to make way for the New Public Safety Building. The new facility would be able to house about seventy inmates. I hope that as I continue, you will get a feel of how I loved the jail ministry.

Love,

Dad

Behind Bars

I grew up scared of the police. If you received a speeding ticket, you paid a $12.50 fine back in the 1930's, and everyone in the community knew how fast you were going. The word got around. I cannot remember when I felt called to a ministry "behind bars." I do know that I was in a worship service and the preacher was preaching from Hebrews 13:1-3.

"Let brotherly love continue. Do not forget to entertain strangers, for by so doing some have unwittingly entertained angels. Remember the prisoners as if chained with them – those who are mistreated – since you yourselves are in the body also."

The writer of the epistle to the Hebrews was giving moral directions to the church. He began by saying, **"Let brotherly love continue."** (V.1) The kind of love one brother has for another. The love we are to display for one another in the Church. It is the word that is used for the City of Philadelphia, "The City of Brotherly Love." The preacher reminded us that we were to "entertain angels." The reference is to Abraham and the Angel of the Lord as they were about to destroy Sodom and Gomorrah. (Genesis 18:1-19:38) Abraham did not know that he was entertaining angels unawares. Often, in our life, there are circumstances that are of the Lord, and we do not recognize them. I recall **"Remember the prisoners as if chained with them."** Some way, I did not get the next four words, **"those who are mistreated,"** until after getting out of the jail ministry in 2003. It was then that I came to realize that those words meant the victims. I did remember, and I did practice the last phrase, **"Since you yourselves are also in the body."** These three verses are still a very real part of my life. I have no troubled loving and caring for a prisoner, no matter what he or she has done. I know that God can fix anything. Thus, as I look to the days immediately ahead of me, I know that God will give me a love that makes a difference for the gay community.

At first, I went to the jail as a pastor. The current chaplain would leave names for me to visit either on the block or in the laundry room. I would get the names and visit. If the visit required tutoring, I would go to the laundry room where we had folding tables to work on. I would tutor in mathematics, write letters, and do anything else that the inmate needed. One of the sergeants, especially, would come down to the laundry room and watch in the window. I could never decide whether he was being cautious or if he did not trust me. I made sure that I was not doing anything that I was not supposed to be doing. Afterwards, I would be debriefed by the undersheriff as to what was accomplished.

My first real challenge came in the fall of 1974. The parents of one of my teenagers came and asked me if I could help their son receive the help that he needed in order to finish his senior year in high school. They told me that their son, Vernon Miner^, had committed arson on a barn and on a garage. I went to the Sheriff and to his school and I setup a program through which I could tutor him. I was permitted to go in on Tuesdays and Thursdays each week. I had to pick up his assignments from the guidance counselor and take them to him. I would tutor him when it was necessary, and I would take his papers and work to the school for corrections. I did this from November 1974 to June 1975. He got out of school in time to take his examinations, to pass, to graduate with his class, and to receive his diploma.

Vernon eventually joined our church, and he is still a member today. I contacted him yesterday to get permission to tell his story, even though I must use a pseudonym per the current Sheriff's instructions, and Vernon shared a very interesting fact. His original charge was grand theft auto. Another interesting fact is that over the years he has become a best friend to my son David. God works in wonderful ways to display his love for us. Was it worth it? Yes, and I pray that our wonderful Lord will be glorified.

The next inmate I want to tell you about is David Blackmore^. I have known David since he was seventeen. Even though I am twice his age, we liked each other from the first. One thing I know is that he is a kleptomaniac as well as an alcoholic. No one wanted him. His mother had remarried, and his name had been changed once again. He was one mixed up kid. Early in 1988, he was getting released from jail and he had no place to go. He had burned his bridges behind him. When I first met him, I told him that someone had stolen my camera. I had left it on the console of my unlocked car, and someone had come along and lifted it. I had no idea that I was talking to the culprit. In about three weeks, David could stand it no longer, and he told me that it was he who had stolen it. He had sold it to a friend for $10.00. He gave me the friend's name, and I got the camera back for the amount of $10.00. Later, the individual would mail the check back to me. He noted that he was afraid that he might be charged with possession of stolen property.

In February of 1988, David was released from Jail and placed on probation. His mother, family, and friends had been burned many times. I asked my wife, June, if he could come and live with us. She graciously agreed. He lived with us for six months. I took him to Alcoholics (AA) meetings all over Wyoming County. You name it, I did it with him. I took him to mental health doctor's appointments and anything else that he was required as a part of probation to do. Part of the deal was that I had to go to AA meetings for non-alcoholics as a part of his therapy. I at least learned firsthand what it was like to attend meetings all the time. Early in September, I took him to an AA Meeting. We came home around 9:30 P.M. He wanted to stop and see his mother, so I dropped him off at the bar where she worked as a bartender. I received a call from the local police asking if my car was in the driveway around 4:30 A.M. the next morning. Naturally, I said that it was. I was asked to check, and when I did, it was not there.

Later, he would tell me that his mother had got him drunk, and she claimed that he had got her drunk. Either way, my white Plymouth was stopped by police on I-400. He had got angry because his mother's boyfriend had misused her. He took my extra set of keys and the car and had tried to run the boyfriend down with my car around his house. He then took off for Buffalo, New York. I had to go and retrieve my car from the Erie County pound. He served another year in jail because of auto theft, since I decided that I would not drop the charges.

After being in and out of jail and rehabilitation programs, David asked me, "May I come and stay with you for three days?" He had been part of a peer training program, and he needed a place to stay. June and I reluctantly agreed that he could come and stay for three days. He arrived on Monday, and on Wednesday, my wife heard him on our phone changing his address to our home. She informed him that he could not do that. He became angry and left the house around 10:00 A.M. He took off, and we heard nothing more from him for the rest of the day. We went to a prayer meeting that evening in my pickup. After the meeting, I stopped and filled up on gas. It was cheaper on Wednesday. I drove into the driveway and parked, wanting to fill June's car as well.

"June where is your car?"

"It is in the garage."

"No, it isn't."

We discovered that he had broken into the house, got the spare keys for her car, and taken off. The next day, he brought the car back into the area and got picked up by the police. We were able to retrieve the car once again. He did not stay at our house after that.

One other inmate who we tried to help was Nate Swain^ in 1991 and 1992. He had been in our local jail and had been transferred to the Clinton Correctional Facility in Dannemora, NY to serve state time. Here again was a young man who had run out of options. June and I had visited him about three times in as many institutions. We travelled to the Clinton Facility to bring him to our home where he stayed for about two months. June and I had decided that we needed to go on vacation, but did not want to leave him in our home alone. On a Tuesday, his parole officer stopped to see how he was doing. June asked the parole officer what we could do with him, and Nate went berserk. The parole officer arrested him. I was at work at the local jail, and June told the parole officer and June that I had molested him. This was not true, but I was immediately placed on administrative leave. The undersheriff, in the meantime, convinced him to admit that it was not true. That did not stop the administrative leave procedure. It was required that I had to appear before my Bishop and Superintendent. I had to obtain a release from the county mental health doctor and from a neutral psychiatric doctor. I was able to go back to work in June of that year after four months of being on leave. My bishop later told me, "You cannot bring inmates into your home. If you cannot do it for everyone, you may not do it for anyone." Since then, I have been obedient to that order.

There are two things that happened concerning Nate. While he was in our home, he had access to my office and files. He had stole documents and had obtained information about our adopted son Myke. He had obtained copies of Myke's social security number, adoption papers, and of other papers that would enable him to establish a new identity. His intent was to go to North Carolina and do just that. I discovered this as I went through his belongings after he went back to jail. I thank God that things turned out like they did. It would have caused Myke a lot of grief, if Nate had gone through with his plans. Before the ordeal was over, Nate wrote me a letter of apology, I would sit with him, and we had a time of reconciliation. He eventually went back upstate, and I have never heard of his whereabouts since then. I can say this one thing about myself: "I am a hard learner."

Learning the Ropes

After ten years, of being out of the chaplaincy, I still listen for a door to latch after me once I go through it. You always had to check to make sure a door was closed for security reasons. If it did not latch, you made sure to find a reason. The security was not only for you, but also for the next one using that door. It may be a correctional officer or an inmate that had ticked another inmate off. As a chaplain, I was able to transport prisoners from one area of the jail to another.

The Attica "uprising" was in 1972. I began prison work just about three years after that incident.

One day early on, we had a big, tall inmate come into the jail. He was about 6 foot 6 inches tall. I was in Two North when he asked me this question:

"Chaplain, what would happen if we took you hostage?"

I told him "Nothing. I told the Sheriff that if anything happened and I was taken hostage, he was not to make any deals. I have been in jail and I know how to handle myself."

I really did have that conversation with the Sheriff. About two weeks later in the same block, that same inmate asked me the same question again. I told him the same thing. I believe he was looking to see if I was scared or bluffing. I was neither scared nor bluffing, and I never had any problems with him after those two instances.

I can remember several challenges that came my way. They happened during a part of the inmate library time. The first was between two forty-something Inmates. There were about four or five other inmates in the library that day. One of those two inmates was bending over, trying to find a book that he wanted, when the other one came up behind him and butted him with his knee right into the stack. Needless to say, I had a problem on my hand. I had to separate them, get help, and restore order. I put one outside the library, calmed the other one down, and called for backup almost in the same breath. I also let them know that they were going to "Keep lock." They did not know it, but I could not put them in keep lock. It was just a common consequence for fighting. They got the point.

Two of the biggest challenges I had in jail ministry came in my work with juveniles and females. I ministered to both effectively, but I found it difficult to develop a rapport with the women. We provided them with the same programs that were available for the men, and on occasion, the programs would appear to run smoothly. Then something would happen and we would have to back up and start all over again.

The juveniles were like all other teenagers. They did not have motivation. They were, for the most part, dropouts from school who had got into trouble and had to learn the hard way. One day, I was having library for about five juveniles. Two of them, I believe, wanted to try me out and to see what I would do. They started a fight and were banging each other's heads on the cement floor. They found out that the old man could take care of them. I separated them and called for backup. The library was cut short that day. Whatever happens in jail not only affects you, but also all the others in your group or block.

Then, there was a day when I had ten or twelve adult males in the library. I did not know it at the time, but some of the inmates were planning to have a rumble in the library. You never know how they will try you out or when they will try to catch you by surprise. One seven foot tall inmate who weighed about three hundred pounds suddenly draped his big arm across my shoulders and announced to the library in general, "The chaplain is my friend." There was no rumble that day. They knew they had to go through Big John^ to try me out and they decided it was not worth the consequences. They knew Big John could take care of himself and me if the situation demanded it. I thank God for all of the friends that I was able to make in jail. Sometimes it paid off when you least expected it. If, I was offered the chance to return to prison ministry today, I would do it in a heartbeat.

Beginning in 1992, the jail housed up to 35 immigration prisoners at a time for the United States Immigration Service. One of my responsibilities was to provide a Friday prayer time, al-jumu 'ah, for Muslim Inmates. I never acted as an Imam, but was there to provide a time of prayer for them. They never once gave me a problem. However, one of the Muslim inmates did not desire my services. He requested that I not pray with him. One day when I was in A-Block, he asked to talk with me. I paused and went over to him, and he asked me to pray with him about his father, who was very sick. I had no trouble laying my hands on his shoulders, bowing our heads together, and praying with him about his father. I thank God for answered prayers. I normally ate with a different block each day when I was in the jail, and it was normal practice for me to pause and pray with anyone who felt the need instead of waiting for the next worship service. The need was now!

I want to thank the good, the bad, and the indifferent for all of the fond memories. I can say that I was watchful, but never unduly concerned about my safety. I loved them, no matter why they were there, and they in turn respected me. Today, if I was to meet some on the street, they would stop and tell me how they are doing, and they would willingly share how good God has been to them and their families. I have baptized some of their children, and for others I have become like a grandpa. I never stop them on the street. I have always tried to respect their privacy and to be sensitive to their needs.

"Rejoice evermore. Pray without ceasing. In everything give thanks for this is the will of God in Christ Jesus concerning you." 1 Thessalonians 5:16-18 (NKJV) *Father, I thank you for the memories. Amen!*

Jail Program Direction

It is one thing to sit across from inmates and have them share their lives with you. You never know how you are going to be received. Often, the feeling is, "I did the crime and now I do the time." At other times, you can be the one person with whom they can let off steam. I have sat in the interview room many times, and I enjoy the challenge and the relationships that begin in an unordinary place and time in life. I have sat often with someone in his cell who needs to think things through when he gets a "Dear John Letter," or who learns that his wife is expecting and that he won't witness the birth. Tears flow and prayers go up, and you pray that somehow you may be able to work a miracle. However, more goes on behind the scenes.

In December of 1991, we were in moved into a brand new seventy cell facility. I had gone into the old jail and ministered on a one-on-one basis, because we did not have the space necessary for any extended program. If the teacher for the education program was there, I was out of there.

I did not have a program booklet or a place where I might get one. What did I have? I had a sheriff that was charged on one hand with the security of the inmate and the jail and on the other hand, a desire to make a difference in the life of the inmate. We had been able to start a Jail Chaplaincy Committee that was advisory to the Sheriff and to whom we reported the activity in the Chaplaincy and the Program on a regular basis. We proceeded to draw up definite guidelines in every area and developed a program that we felt needed to be in place.

The Jail Committee was formed by pastors and laymen and laywomen of different faiths in the community. They provided the means to have an ongoing ministry in the Jail. They provided Bibles and materials that were not available through the state, and they recommended men and women who could be used for the various programs. There were about sixty to seventy people who were involved in this ministry. The volunteers had to apply, to be recommended by my office, and to be approved by the Jail Chaplaincy Committee. The Sheriff and the Undersheriff sat on this committee.

The various programs that were set up and worked into a time schedule were as follows:

- All spiritual, educational, recovery programs (including Alcoholics Anonymous)
- Mental health case management
- Social Services made available to the inmate or detainee
- The volunteer program that made many of the programs feasible.

The spiritual program was relatively easy. The chaplain met with the inmate soon after entry into the jail. If he or she desired to see a pastor, we would call their pastor and inform them of the inmate's desire. The spiritual aspect included Bible Study, Chaplain's Hour (Prayer), and worship services much like those you would find in the local church community. The chaplain was the coordinator for all programming. There was a Bible Study each week by a community pastor, and every Saturday the Local Camp of Gideon's International would come to give the layman a chance to be involved in the Chaplaincy. The Chaplain provided the regular Sunday Worship Service for those desiring to attend. The Local Camp of The Gideon's International was set in place for each Saturday morning at 9:30 A.M. They were laymen who provided and distributed Bibles to the inmates as well as having a Bible Study for them on a weekly basis. They provided the inmates with role models of how Christian men should function. There were several of them who would come in for Lay Bible Studies and take a month every Thursday for an hour.

The Educational Program was provided by BOCES. Therefore, the program met state standards. The Teacher was a tenured teacher. She provided programs for High School students, and for all Adult educational programs. When a Teen was in the Facility the Teacher would contact his school teacher and guidance counselor and he/she would continue on with his/her education. They worked together in order that the Inmate might conclude his education successfully. She also provided the Adult Education Program. They needed someone to give the General Educational Development (GED) tests in the Facility. I became certified as a Chief Examiner for the New York State GED program and whenever the Teacher had Inmates that were ready for testing I would give the tests and return them to the New York State Department of Education for correcting and for them to give a GED diploma. We had about an eighty percent graduation rate. I was not allowed to do any of the teaching of the students since I was the Chief Examiner.

The other programs that came into the jail were set up for the providing agency so that the agency had clearance to see inmates. Each person had to submit an application, and the dates and times had to be agreed upon. The Program Director worked as a liaison between the jail and the various organizations.

We had to make arrangements for Alcoholics Anonymous (AA) to come in on a regular basis for those who needed help to overcome alcohol and drugs. These twelve step programs helped the inmates to come to grips with their needs before hitting the streets again and experiencing all the uncertainty that came along with reintegration. They became somewhat familiar with programs that were available to help them live successfully in society again.

Mental health services had to be provided when they were court ordered or when individuals obviously needed help. The program director would interview an inmate and get his/her permission to contact the Mental Health Department. As program director, I would then meet with Mental Health to determine what type of program was needed to meet the individual's needs. It was also my responsibility to contact the inmate and keep up with his or her status so that the court's and Mental Health Department's recommendations were followed. It was at times very tedious and trying to get everything done so that the individual could return to the community.

One duty that proved extremely important was making contact with the Department of Social Services so that inmates would have something to live on after exiting the facility, especially if he or she no longer had employment available. Applications needed to be made 42 days before the exit date. There were times when inmates had no place to stay. It was at this point that Social Services and I scurried to find suitable places for inmates to live. As I look back, it was challenging to put the pieces together, and at the same time it was very rewarding. Yes, I made mistakes, and sometimes I did not have the time to put all the pieces together. However, I tried to accomplish the goal of returning someone to a worthwhile life. I also made it my goal to appreciate the privilege of leading one more inmate to the Lord Jesus Christ and for him/her to experience the joy of knowing the love of God for all eternity.

One of the needs that became apparent was recognition for the volunteer program. There were about seventy unpaid volunteers, and the Jail Chaplaincy Committee set in place an Annual Dinner to award those who had done a great job. The first one was held on November 9, 1995, and it was held at the high school, as best as I can remember. We had a catered dinner with all of the Thanksgiving decorations, and after nineteen years, the banquet is still an annual program, including special music and a message challenging those present with some phase of jail ministry. As a climax, the volunteers are recognized.

My first accolade came on February 23, 1978, when the local Camp of Gideon's International presented me with a Bible for those who had been active in the community. There were times when I spoke at other jail facilities for their volunteers. I have no way of knowing all the times I have been thanked for my contribution to the community through my work in jail ministry, hospital chaplaincy, and nursing homes. I appreciate all their ways of saying "Thank you, and well done." I, in turn, say with a very grateful and thankful heart, "Thank you." The last time I was recognized was in February 2004, after I had retired from being jail chaplain. The Gideon's once again gave me a VEEP Bible, and I received a plaque and a declaration of appreciation for ministry well done from the then Sheriff of Wyoming County, New York. Would I do it again? "Yes," I can answer with tear-filled eyes, as I look back with deep appreciation for what my wonderful God has done through me.

PART FIVE: CHRISTIAN MINISTRY

I have never won an argument with God. His loving grace went before me as I argued and could not understand how He would want me. I had done all the wrong things. Finally, He won. "Lord, give me the faith to believe you want me." He did! A year later, He gave me a call to pastoral ministry. Again, I argued, "Lord, I have cursed, smoked, drank, divorced, sexed, and I could keep going." My loving Savior won that battle as well. He snookered me into serving Him in jail ministry. I have spent 33 years as chaplain. Then, my son Michael came out to his mother and me on November 15, 1987. God called me to a ministry to the gay community. I tried, but things did not work out. He called me to write my autobiography. We argued over that for at least fifteen years. For the last two and a half years, I have been sick. Finally, I said yes. Now you know the story. My loving Triune God had won again! I do not know how He will open up my final years of ministry to the LGBT Community. That is the rest of the story. I do know that, once again, He will win!

Letter to Myke

Dear Son,

I have examined every area of my life through this writing process, and as I have examined, there has been joy at times when laughter could be heard over the noise of the keyboard. Tears have flowed freely many times. I have had strong desires to ask for forgiveness, even when that is no longer possible. In that case, I have looked into my imaginary mirror of my life and have not liked what I have seen. It is at those moments that I put into practice what Christ has done for me, and I forgive myself just as He has forgiven me. I have this task to complete, after I have completed my biography: to visit with each one of my children to somehow show them my contrition and at the same time express my love for each of them.

I am thinking about the presence of homosexuality in each area of my life. I was born with it. I know at least three times that it surfaced before I went to first grade. It was there in fantasy in grades one through four. It was there in actuality during grades five through eight. Moving and changing school districts in no way changed my desire. Throughout high school and during my naval service it was there. The thread has been there the entire time I have been a Christian. Integrity and faithfulness have survived the attacks of Satan. There were times when I was a breath away from succumbing to the temptation. Jesus provided a way of escape. I thank God! The tapestry of my life will end in a ministry to the lesbian, gay, bisexual, and transgendered (LGBT) community. The finished tapestry, figuratively speaking, will lay a life well-lived at the feet of Jesus. I will crown Him with it as the "Lord of Lords and King of Kings," and I will begin to praise Him for all Eternity.

Myke, you are going to have to wade through my Christian views and how I have found that they have worked in my life. The gay lifestyle and faith do not appear, to me, to go together. However, I feel that God has a plan for each of us. He made His plan work for the early Church, and He will make it work for us today. I did not call myself to this ministry. God called me just as surely as He called me into the Pastoral and Jail ministry.

I want to list the final chapters of my book. There first is this letter to you. The second will be about how I got to where I am at the present time. The third will be about my Conservative Wesleyan Armenian point of view. The fourth will show you my stubborn attitude and how God dealt with it. My vision for the future will be explained, and I will close my autobiography with a vision for future ministry in the epilogue. I will provide selected Biblical topics such as love, anger, stubbornness, etc. They will be entitled Biblical Study Guides, and they should be very helpful for a one-on-one approach to individuals or to group ministry in any setting. They should be helpful to anyone reaching out to the gay community. I feel they should be helpful to anyone that is looking for a personal individual study. Finally, I have decided to provide a selected bibliography.

Love,

Dad

Writing My Autobiography

It really began back in 1988. God gave me a glimpse of what a ministry to the LGBT community could look like at Marketplace Mall. It could have taken place in the central area, and we could have had a worship service each Sunday and been able to provide a ministry throughout the week by visiting people in the mall with the message of salvation. Several things hindered that vision. First, I simply did not want to do it. Secondly, I did not want to be known as Mr. Homosexuality. Lastly, I did not know how to accomplish it. I was stubborn and I fought it. I retired and it was like putting it on the back burner.

Bill Jr. asked me to address his "Men of Integrity" group at Ransomville Free Methodist Church. I felt he wanted me to bring a message of challenge to his men on Sunday morning, June 1 2003, at 8:00 A.M. No, he wanted me to give my personal testimony. I reluctantly agreed. There were about 30 men at that breakfast. What I did not realize was that two of my grandsons would be sitting at the front table staring me in the eyes. They were about 16 and 18 at that time. It was a challenge, but I got through it. That was not the end. My oldest Grandson visited me on December 28th. He gave me a gift of a long muffler and made a request. He said, "Poppy you have to write your autobiography." I agreed, and told him, "If I do not finish it, you have to finish it." The Lord willing he won't have to do it.

I would stop and start. I was fighting myself. I was fighting the Lord. I did not want to reveal to anyone who or what I was. I grew up in a culture where, if someone found you out, you would end up in a back alley and you would get the beating of your life, many times by the local police. I had a friend who I spent a great deal of time with. We went to clam bakes, drank, and we would wrestle or fool around. One time I was thinking of approaching him. I am glad I did not do so. About a month later, someone did approach him, and he beat the person up. He was arrested for attempted manslaughter and did time in jail. I thank God for the times that He has protected me. Even though I had promised, I stubbornly refused to write meaningfully.

God finally had enough of my stubbornness. On July 11, 2011, I had asked to be consecrated as Chaplain to the Gay Community by our Endorsing Agent. I knew I needed to write, but that did not move me out of my attitude. In the late fall of 2011, my health took a turn for the worse. I would go to the doctor and get an antibiotic, and it would help for a little while. Added to this, I had, in my sophomore year of high school, dropped a lead hammer on my right big toe. The nail was always deformed. I had trouble with bronchitis. Now, added to that, I lost my right big toe nail. I got ulcers on my feet. I got infection in my feet. I developed fungus infection all over my body. Every crack I looked at there was fungus infection. I had three doctors, and they could not get a hold on the problem. I spent the spring of 2012 in my lounge chair with my feet off the floor giving myself daily antibiotic shots for the infection for six weeks.

On December 11, 2012, I went to my granddaughter's 7th grade Christmas concert. It was cold. As I walked into her school, I began experiencing severe breathing problems. I thought it was the cold air. The next day when I went the doctor, he told me I was having heart problems. He immediately sent me to the hospital emergency room. I am not going into all the details, but during the next six months I would be in a hospital six times. I was assigned six specialists to treat each area of my symptoms. My medication list was out of control. I had gone from 167 to 223 pounds in weight. I was a "Buddha" because I was filled with fluid. I could hardly get myself out of bed or a chair. Three times, I came one breath away from my last breath. Each time, there was no one with me. I was at home alone. I stopped breathing. I had been lying on my side and someone hit my left shoulder, and suddenly I was on my back gasping. I managed to get to the bathroom and started breathing again. The same scenario played out during two different stays at the hospital. No one was in the room. I quit breathing, I got hit, and I started breathing again. On May 21st at my son's home, I passed out and his wife who is a nurse told me that I was almost gone. God watches out for those He calls to serve Him.

This section will end as I finish the story of my life. I went to a camp meeting the first week of July 2013. I did *not* want to go, but I had nowhere else I could go. That does not mean I was happy. The more the evangelist preached the more miserable I became. At the close of Tuesday's message, I went and threw myself on the altar in complete submission. I was totally exhausted. I believe that if I had not gone that evening, I would have been dead today. I came home with new vision. I started writing. The fungus is gone. I have no infection. I have no cracks, the last time I checked. I check daily. And, I am within sixty days of submitting my book to the printers. The Lord does not care how miserable you get. He wants your obedience.

My Wonderful Lord has reminded me many times of the following verse: **"For rebellion is as the sin of witchcraft, and stubbornness is as iniquity and idolatry."** (1 Samuel 15:23 KJV) I was stubborn admittedly so. The Holy Spirit has helped me deal with that. God has forgiven me for Christ's sake. My health is returning. I am in the will of God currently. I lift my praise to a great Triune God.

His will is my will. He has called me to be a chaplain to the gay community. I wholeheartedly accept the greatest challenge of my life without reserve from Jesus Christ.

It Works

"How beautiful are the feet of those who preach the Gospel of peace; who bring glad tidings of good things." *(Romans 10:15B)*

I have been in pastoral ministry for sixty years. I retired from the active ministry twenty-three years ago in 1991. I served as a Jail Chaplain for twenty-nine years, retiring in 2003. I have been a widower for 7 years. About ten years ago, I was asked to be the Congregational Care Pastor at the Church where I worshipped. I minister on a volunteer basis and subsequently was appointed by my Conference to be Pastor Emeritus. This means I can minister at the discretion of the local pastor to do anything that I could do as an active pastor. For a time I lived alone, without even a pet, but I was not lonely. Once in a while, I would yell at myself just to hear someone talk.

I kept office hours four days a week from 9:00 – 12:00 P.M. give or take a little bit here and there. I filled my afternoons with ministry to the community. I was on call 24/7 at the local Hospital for emergencies; and there I visited patients on a regular basis. I also visited at the jail with inmates that were a part of our church or who had been referred to me by their families. I preached once a month at a local Nursing Home and gave them communion. I visited them and I was available to help meet their needs.

Two years ago, a friend kept after me to go out to breakfast with him. His wife passed away about three months before mine did. Each week on my day off, which is Thursday, we go out to breakfast. Lantz's Bulk Foods is a great place to get a good farmer's breakfast at a very reasonable price. They have several good choices. Mine is No. 5. It includes two eggs over easy, hash browns, a choice of bacon, sausage or ham, and choice of toast (wheat, rye, salt rising, etc.), and, as the waitress comes to my table she has my free decaf coffee in her hand. After dumping one creamer in the cup I am off. Do you want to join me next Thursday? Our group at breakfast is sometimes two and at other times it can be eight. We live in a rural redneck conservative community and the makeup of our group reflects that culture.

You need a little more background. I am a man of prayer. I have a foster son that is serving the Lord in New Mexico in camping ministries. I have prayed for him for about fifty years. I have prayed for one of my friends who served time for over seventeen years. I had the privilege of leading him to Christ in the local jail. I have four special friends and families that I want to see come to the Lord. I have a son that is gay and living in Rochester, NY. I need to be a man of prayer. I want you to know that once you get on my list, you never get off of it. I have been praying for those men who I eat breakfast with. All of them are not Christians, and they come from different church backgrounds. The conversations range all over the spectrum of life. Once in a long while, opportunity will arise and they get preached to. They accept it. They occasionally ask me to pray for their individual needs.

Two months ago, Grant^ quietly asked me to pray for his wife, Sandy ^ and he told me that no one knew yet that his wife had just been diagnosed with throat cancer. She has since had surgery and is facing chemotherapy and radiation simultaneously for her ongoing treatment. A week ago, Sandy's^ sister asked me to make a hospital visit. Sandy has been a Christian all of her life. Grant had not made that commitment during about 44 years of their being married. I saw Sandy for about a minute, and because of treatment it was off to the waiting room. Another friend who was with me helped me share the Gospel with Grant. Grant told us about being in Vietnam during his stay in the Army. He said, "I promised the Lord if I got out of there I would serve Him." He never kept that commitment for over 45 years.

I had made a like commitment when I was in the Navy, sixty years ago. I shared my life with Grant. He expressed a desire to make the commitment that he had promised God, years before. We prayed and shared our faith with each other. We shared Grant's decision to be a Christian with Grant's brother-in-law and his wife. Finally, I was allowed another minute to tell Sandy that her prayers of 43 years were answered and to give a brief prayer of Thanksgiving for Grant's salvation and her healing.

I thought this morning about what happened on that day, and suddenly the Scripture from Romans 10:15B was made real to me. I pictured preachers in Biblical times walking from place to place with either bare feet or sandals, and I could suddenly **understand "How beautiful are the feet of those who preach the Gospel of peace."** Then, I asked this question, "Are my feet beautiful where the leather meets the pavement?" Yes, being a Christian works!

Father, help us to build bridges into our community over which non-Christians can walk. Help each one of us to eat breakfast and to smell the roses with friends until they are able to cross the bridges we are building into their world and they will be able to say, **"How beautiful are the feet of them where leather meets the pavement."** *Amen!*

Pastoral Ministry

The strands of my life and my ministry are in extricable linked. They are interwoven like the plaiting of a lady's hair. My life is my ministry. My ministry is my life. They are inseparable. The unlovely has been turned into a tapestry of beauty. The 26 years of living in sin, of being bi-sexual, of being an alcoholic, in all their ugly black darkness have been woven into the tapestry of my life. Sixty-two years of living as a Christian, of serving the Lord Jesus Christ, and the several ministries in which I serve display bright colors which have also been interwoven into a final portrait of beauty.

The years from 1954 to 1964 were somewhat spotty. The Lord allowed me twelve years to get major things in place in my life. Though the ministry appears to be intermittent, the emptiness was filled with teaching Sunday school classes in the churches that we attended, in prayer meetings that we lead, and in leadership that we provided as a layman. In addition to this, there were Sundays that were filled with supply preaching for nearby churches and pastors, and, there were times that we supplied evangelistic services in our conference or in community churches.

I was not alone in my ministry. Violet was a great Christian. She had taken courses before we were married in order that she could lead in Christian Education Ministries. She could lead singing and participate in the life of the church in a very meaningful way. In early June of 1962, she told me that she was going to a Christian CYC camp to be craft director. She did not ask. Her mind was made up. The camp was in early July. She encouraged me to come to camp in the evenings after work to be a senior counselor for eight teenage boys. At least six of them, as they matured, would become pastors. Our ministry was then, and continued over the years to be fruitful. I have been in full-time ministry from November 1964 until the present as a full time pastor. I cannot sing. However, I could follow Violet as she sang the hymns that were picked out. I learned to follow her lead. I loved to have her sing special songs.

The last time that I was able to communicate with her was just before she lost her battle with cancer. We read Psalm 23, and she sang very quietly, "Wonderful, Wonderful, Jesus." The chorus goes *"Wonderful, Wonderful Jesus, In the heart He implanteth a song: A song of deliverance, of courage, of strength, In the ear He implanteth a song."* We prayed together for the last time.

One time when I was a teen, I asked my father how long Lowery's lived. I remember him telling me that the men lived to be 55 or 56 years old. He lived until he was almost 62. My Father was a big man. I always wanted to be bigger than he was. It never happened. I was four inches shorter than he was. My average weight has been over the years about eighty pounds lighter. However, when I was sixty two, I beat him in longevity, and I am still counting.

As a young Christian, I often thought about what he had told me. I was heart-broken that I had wasted all those years and maybe had only 30 more years to live. I cried about the fact and I prayed. You will like the Lord's arithmetic. I have had sixty years of pastoral ministry. I enjoyed 27 years of camping ministry. Though I only served less than three months in a US Naval Brig, I served 33 years in jail doing a Chaplain's ministry. Long ago I lost count as to how many inmates ended up as Christians. Currently, I correspond with about five former or current inmates. During the interim of 1972-2012, I served at Wyoming County Community Hospital for forty years as a Pastor, Chaplain or a Spiritual Life Volunteer doing those various ministries. I will do the math for you. It adds up to 160 years. I will admit that, other than the pastoral ministry, the others were fit into my schedule. However, they were served continuously. The length of my days was approximately eighteen hours long. I have served my time and I am still counting and serving it, though the days have been shortened recently to about eight hours.

Time would fail me to tell you all the years of my pastoral ministry. However, may I have the privilege of sharing with you a few highlights? I had a man in the Olean church that would always turn me off when I ministered to him and his sister. I would visit them and read a portion of Scripture, but very seldom would he want me to pray with him, or he would turn me off entirely. He would charge his sister who was a brittle diabetic to visit her in the hospital. One time he was in the hospital, and she asked me to visit him. He was not too cooperative. I decided that I would bid him a good night and leave. As I was leaving his room, he challenged me, "Aren't you going to read and pray for me?" I did and I lead him to the Lord. Later, as I would go by their house I would see him on his front porch reading his Bible and praying. He would wave his hand, where before he would have ignored me. He was never able to get to Church following his sickness. However, when I called we shared what Christ had done in his life.

One time I was visiting an elderly lady in the Wyoming County Community Hospital. I had never met her before, and I was not sure what I should do. I read Psalm 46. Before I could pray or say anything to her, she asked, "Could you lead me to Christ?" I did and I prayed with her. I had not seen her before and before I got back, she had left the hospital. How thankful that I followed her request and the leading of the Lord. I have long since forgotten her name, but not the occasion. I praise the Lord!

On another occasion I was in Wyoming County Jail. I had prepared a Bible Study for the Chaplain's Hour. Only one inmate showed up. I felt sorry for myself. I had worked hard. I sat down with him and I did the Bible Study. He was a very shy young man. I had the privilege to lead him to faith in Christ. If there had been one other person there, I would not have had the chance to lead him to Christ. I learned to follow the leading of the Holy Spirit in my ministry.

My desire is not to blow my own horn. My goal is permit you to see behind the curtain of my life, to see what my ministry has been like, and to help you visualize how God has used me in ministry. I have had some challenging churches to pastor. I have served ten separate congregations. Each one has presented a different challenge. In one church, I had three men tell me on their separate front lawns, "I will be watching you." Needless to say, for the first year I very seldom went anywhere without one of my children or some other person with me. Before I left that church, it had grown from about 35 to about 85. It was a healthy church.

I pastored one church where, on the third Sunday I preached, a non-member told me, "We do not use the Doxology in our Church." After six years the Church was growing. I had received an 84% vote to be reassigned to the church as pastor. I was elated. However, about ten days before the Bishop was to make pastoral assignments, my Superintendent told me that I would be moving to a church that was in trouble. The new church grew. It is not always the church or the congregation that causes change. Often, change comes from other sources and sometimes from family. My fourth wife had been in pastoral and camping ministry about thirty years with her previous husband. Her idea for a camping ministry was the Waldorf Astoria with a good thick shag rug on the flour and all the amenities that go with it. Therefore, after prayer from both of us about not doing camping ministry, I resigned from my position as camp director in 1989. God was leading.

Around that time, God put on my heart to begin a ministry to the gay community. I worked on it with the Marketplace mall as the site of Sunday worship services. It never materialized. As I look back, I am thankful that it did not come to fulfillment. I look forward and I know that God will bring about a ministry to the lesbian, gay, bi-sexual, and transgendered (LGBT).

Statement of Personal Faith

I believe the Bible, the Word of God, from cover to cover. In begins with, "In the beginning God created the Heavens and the earth." (Genesis 1:1 NKJV) It ends with Jesus and the Apostle John in dialogue. Listen! "[Jesus] who testifies to these things says, 'Surely I am coming quickly.'" The Apostle John responds to the Lord, "Amen! Even so, come, Lord Jesus!" Then, the Apostle pronounces a benediction on the Seven Churches and, I believe, on believers for all time. "The grace of our Lord Jesus Christ be with you all. Amen!" (Revelation 22:20-21 NKJV) I believe all that is in between the "In the beginning God," and the final word, "Amen". I drop this quote to emphasize my viewpoint: "God says it; I believe it; that settles it."

I am Wesleyan Armenian in regards to my theological view point. I believe in salvation by faith. I believe that a believer can be sanctified by being baptized and cleansed through the Holy Spirit from the sinful carnal nature of man. Personally, I can embrace "The Apostle's Creed" as my affirmation of faith. I will be listing the 2011 Book of Discipline of the Free Methodist Church in my Selected Bibliography. This will enable you to understand my faith and the position of the Church I serve with regards to marriage and any issues that may arise in your life and to understand especially the diversity of sexuality in the culture in which we live and exercise our faith.

The Church is divided into many different branches. We know that we have Catholics and Protestants. We understand that we have Roman Catholics and Eastern Orthodox Catholic churches and others of Catholic backgrounds. We know that we have Calvinists, Wesleyan Armenians, and Pentecostal believers that would class themselves as Protestant. I have listed these so that you may become familiar with them and to help you be able to do research as to where you stand in regards to your personal belief and to what your church believes.

I was ordained Deacon in July of 1969 at our Annual Conference. After meeting all of my requirements for Elders Orders, I was ordained Elder on August 2, 1972, by Bishop Edward C. John. I took those vows very seriously. I affirm that I have lived in integrity and faithfulness to those vows, and it is my purpose to continue to live by the vows that I took on that date.

I am between a rock and a hard place. I know what I believe. I think I understand what the LGBT culture believes. "I was born with that orientation." I have heard great "Men of faith" contradict that statement. They say that those identifying as homosexual either have a predisposition to being gay or that it is learned behavior. Now, which of the three is it? I desire to define my personal beliefs, and from them, I will continue to write what I believe God wants me to say in my autobiography. I want you to realize that this is not a research paper. It is the story of my life as told by me.

I have used online resources, my dictionary, theology books and commentaries to come to a clear position of what I believe. I have read books without number. I have left filed a cabinet of collected articles that I have collected about the different problems that exist when you mention the gay community. Succinct definitions will follow. My goal is to provide simple definitions that anyone can understand. Also, I want to leave behind biblical and theological words. "KISS" might be a good idea. "Keep it Simple, Stupid." I will try!

Definitions

DNA – is a molecule that encodes the genetic instructions used in the development and functioning of all living organisms and many viruses." (Wikipedia Encyclopedia)[3]

Sexual – (Adj.) pertaining to sex, sexual relations[4]

---

[3] DNA definition source
[4] Random House Webster's College Dictionary. (2000). New York, NY. Random House.

Orientation – (n) is the process of orientating, the attainment of one's true position, as in a novel situation. Orientation is the general direction of or tendency of one's approach, thoughts, etc.[5]

Predispose – (v) is to make susceptible or liable; is to forgive or furnish a tendency or inclination.[6]

Celibate – (n) is a person that abstains from sexual relations; a person who remains unmarried especially for religious purposes.[7]

Carnal Mind – We (the Church and I) believe in salvation through faith in the Lord Jesus Christ. Thereby, I become a "believer". We call this the "Atonement" (Uh-tōn-mint) with Christ. We believe that the Holy Spirit cleanses us from the carnal mind. The "Carnal Mind" is often referred to as inbred sin or the carnal nature. I would say, "The nature that I was born with." (See Dr. H.O. Wiley, Intro. To Christian Theology, page 253)[8]

For me, DNA is out. Sexual orientation is iffy, unless you call it a "novel situation." The carnal nature or inbred sin appears to fit that which I have experienced. I will have to agree that I have had a predisposition to a bisexual orientation and that learned behavior can be a conditioned response or stimuli through either voluntary or involuntary intent or acts. I affirm that the carnal nature, a predisposition, and learned behavior were all factors in my life. How does this equate with living and serving God as a Christian minister? However, I have lived a celibate or heterosexual lifestyle as a believer in Christ.

This is my "Statement of Faith." It is how I have lived out what I believe?

---

[5] Ibid.
[6] Ibid.
[7] Random House Webster's College Dictionary. (2000). New York, NY: Random House.
[8] Wiley, H.O., (1954). The dispensation of the Holy Spirit. In H.O. Wiley and P.T. Culbertson, *Introduction to Christian Theology* (253). Kansas City, Missouri: Beacon Hill Press.

Living Out My Faith

I firmly believe that I was born with inbred sin or a carnal nature. At four pounds and four ounces, I was a sinner. I can hear my mother say to my father, "Isn't he a little Angel?" My grandparents, aunts, and uncles did not dare to dispute the fact. They agreed. The fact was that I was born a sinner.

No one had to teach me how to sin. At two and a half years old, I kept biting a two-year-old friend in Clermont, New Hampshire until he got angry and bit my nose until the blood squirted. That biting was sin at work. I learned a lesson. I do not like to be bitten to this day. It makes me angry. No one taught me to have temper tantrums. I am sure my mother never taught me that. My father, on the other hand, taught me that it was not a good thing to lie. I can still feel his hand on my southbound end.

In Eve's words, God told Adam and Eve this: "We may eat of the fruit of the trees of the garden, but of the fruit of the tree which is in the midst of the garden, God has said, 'You shall not eat of it, nor shall you touch it, lest you die.'" (Genesis 3:2-3 NKJV) They ate of the tree of the knowledge of good and evil. If they had obeyed, they would have lived forever in the Garden of Eden, and as a part of the carnal nature, death and dying passed onto all people. The diseases that we have today are a part of the death and dying process. I firmly believe that my gay lifestyle was equally apart of the carnal nature. Unforgiven, it would have led me to Hell.

Jesus can forgive me my sins, and He did! He could not forgive me of my carnal nature. He set the rules. However, He did provide a way of escape. He provided us with His Holy Spirit that can cleanse us from all sin. I believe that He has forgiven me from all the sins I have ever committed. I equally believe that the Holy Spirit has cleansed me from that inbred sin and will continue to do so until the day that I enter into the Holiness of Heaven. In simple words, "I am a work in progress."

I could not believe that God wanted a person that was as sinful as I was. My prayer of faith was simple. "Lord, give me the faith to believe that You want me." He did, and He still does. I wrestled with my sinful nature for over a year. If I did not watch, I would take His name in vain in a fit of anger. The air was filled with all kinds of nasty words. I had asked him to "Turn me every way but loose, that I wanted to know that He had baptized me His Your Holy Spirit and had made me clean." God used "Now faith is the substance of things hoped for; the evidence of thing not seen," to baptize me with His Holy Spirit and to cleanse my heart. I was filled with His joy for about seven hours. I really praised God as I walked up and down Jockey Street in Houghton, New York in February 1954. Laughter filled my soul. At about 5:00 AM, I went to my room with my hand over my mouth to help me to keep from praising Him. I needed sleep.

There are three Scripture lessons I have used to lead individuals to Christ and to help them begin to walk Spirit-filled lives. They are Psalm 24, John 3:1-16, and I John 1:1-10. I will do a "Bible Study Guide" that you may use to lead someone into faith in Christ and into a walk of Godliness. See the Bible Study Guides at the end of my autobiography.

The battle is not won when you receive Christ as your Savior. The sanctifying work of the Holy Spirit is not over when you become baptized with the Holy Spirit. The battle and the work will have just begun. Satan will always know where he can tempt you. God has provided a way to escape those times of temptation.

I have learned that there are places that I should not go. I do not go to those places. I do not drink, because I had problems and I drank, and because I drank, I had problems. It was the same old merry-go-round. I say a simple "No" when I see something that I should not be watching. Likewise, I turn off the TV when the program is raunchy. Pornography is out, especially where men are concerned. Satan knows about my being bisexual. I am a man, and I functioned about forty percent heterosexually. You can surmise what caught my attention the other sixty percent of the time. Remember, I have been married four times. Since my wives have passed away, I have practiced celibacy. The "No" is simple. The living out a life of faith is work!

My challenge is to stop looking at the now and start looking toward the future. I know that I can't do it by myself. The Apostle Paul penned these words: **"I can do all things through Christ which strengthens me."** (Philippians 4:13 NKJV) You and I can experience Paul's affirmation in each of our lives. We can draw Godly strength from that. I can't! God can! It works. Praise God!

Living Out Liberty

"For freedom Christ has made us free; stand fast therefore, and do not be entangled again in the yoke of bondage." (Marginal rendering, Galatians 5:1 NKJV)

I grew up in a very conservative, rural Christian community. I was not permitted to use foul language until after I was eighteen. The first time I heard the word "homosexual," I was about fifteen. The word was hissed at me. I did not like it then, and I still do not. The communities where I grew up would have never accepted anyone "coming out" even to their family. Some things you kept to yourself. I received Christ as my Savior on November 18, 1952. I was forgiven of the sins I had committed, but I did not share with anyone what I was at my very core.

I told the Lord that if He wanted anyone to know why I was in Jail, I would tell them. The first time that happened was in 1978. I have been asked directly maybe about ten times. I have kept that promise for sixty-two years. As I have been writing I have shared much more frequently. I used to scream in the quietness of my being, I want to be "**ME!**"

There are some who have known for years that I am gay. As I have shared with them the content of what I am writing, I get negative responses from family members and from friends. "You are not that now!" But, I live with the knowledge that I was born with a carnal nature. "You can write under a pseudonym!" Yep, I could, but how would it bring glory to God if I hid behind a false name? It would slam me back into the closest even farther. "Have you considered how this will affect your family?" Yes, I have, and I have asked them about the problem. In turn, they have given me their support to do what God has asked me to do. My son asked me to testify to what God had done for me. I did! Two of my grandsons, after hearing that witness, told me, "Poppy, you have to write your autobiography." I am!

I have laughed and chuckled with joy as I have written. I have hung my head in shame, with tears running down my cheeks onto the keyboard. I have dealt with my stubborn nature. I have asked God to forgive me. He did! Where the person has gone into Heaven, and I am unable to ask their forgiveness; I read Colossians 3:13 and I claim it, "Just as Christ has forgiven me," and I forgive myself through faith in Christ's promises. As I write, I find the liberty that has made me free, and I can exclaim to the world, "I am living out liberty, and He has set me free to be me."

The Apostle Paul pens these words of caution, and at the same time words of liberty, and a word of service. **Brethren, you have been called to liberty; only do not use liberty as an opportunity for the flesh, but through love serve one another."** (Galatians 5:13 NKJV) The preacher in me notes an outline for this verse. First, "You have been called to liberty." Second, "You do not use liberty as an opportunity of the flesh," and third, "Through love you serve one another."

First, I thank God that I am living out liberty, and I am able to witness to everyone what God has done in my life. Secondly, I am thankful for the warning not to use liberty for my own gratification. Jesus has saved me from my sin, but I am not to return back to and from what He saved me. And lastly, I praise the Triune God (Father, Son, and Holy Spirit) that He has called me to minister to those caught up in any sin, and especially to the lesbian, gay, bisexual, and transgendered (LGBT). I praise Him, and I welcome the challenge.

I have served God as a Christian, as a pastor, as a jail chaplain, as a spiritual life volunteer, and as chaplain in a hospital setting. I have served the local Church in nearly every position that is available. You name it, and I have probably done it. Now, in love, I go to show that love of God to the LGBT. I do not hate the carnal nature that God gave me and that which He has cleansed. I can say, "What God has done for me, he can do for you." I can say, "God, the Church, and I love you." I am praying for the chance to minister to my world in a very different manner as a Chaplain to the lost, no matter who they may be.

How, what, when and where poses the questions that are ahead of me. The "how" has already been answered. He wanted me to write my autobiography as the means to get a message of love out into my world.

"Who" has also already been answered! It is for anyone that reads my autobiography and needs answers. He wanted me to accept the challenge of loving everyone, and that includes me. Not just some.

Looking to the Future

I ask this question as I look at my future: "Where to, Lord?" I could not believe in 1952 that God really wanted me. It took a tour in the US Naval Brig to bring me to Him by faith. It took a Baptist Missionary saying, "Mister, I have never seen such a sour- lemony pickled-faced puss in all my life. If I were you, I would do something about it" to accept the call to pastoral ministry. It has taken the last ten years to get my autobiography written. In the last two and a half years, He has taken me through rough times with health issues, until I would say, "Yes" and get the task completed. He has shown me that in my soul, I was a stubborn and a hardhearted man. Today I pray that I may be putty in His loving hand.

I have concerns. I tell Him in my own way, and in no uncertain terms, that I am nigh on 88. He quietly reminds me that Moses was 80 when He called him to lead the children of Israel out of Egypt and that Caleb was 85 when he asked Joshua to give him Hebron as his inheritance that had been promised by Moses. I say this reverently: "Jesus doesn't listen too well to me." But, He does not want me to be stubborn or to be hardhearted. He wants me to be obedient to Him, and I desire with all of my heart that I will not stray from obedience in the future.

When I have published The Bush Still Burns, God will have to lead in every step of the way. Primarily, I see a one-on-one ministry. This does not negate a broader ministry to the LGBT community. My prayer is that anyone having issues, hurts, habits, or hang-ups may come to see that God and the Church really do love them in spite of their lifestyle or circumstances. Jesus died for the sins of all the people for all time and for all of life's situations. I want Myke to know that I love him no matter what. I want the world to know that the Church and I love them no matter what. I know what the Bible says, and I believe that God is against all types of sin. Also, I want them to know that God so loved that He gave His only begotten Son that they might be saved from their sins. (John 3:16 NKJV) I want them to know that Christ so loved the world, that he came to die for them. **"By this we know love, because He laid down His life for us. And, we also ought to lay down our lives for the brethren."** (1 John 3:16) The last half of that verse leads us to consider "The Great Commission".

"And Jesus came and spoke to them, saying, "All authority has been given to Me in heaven and on earth. Go therefore and make disciples of all the nations, baptizing them in the name of the Father and of the Son and of the Holy Spirit, teaching them to observe all things that I have commanded you; and lo, I am with you always, even to the end of the age." Amen. All means "All!"

My goal is to ask all men, no matter what their status in life may be. No matter their orientation and no matter their circumstances in life, I want them to know that God loves them, that the Church loves them, and that I love them, and that our love for them is unconditional. My goal is to ask each one that I personally come in contact with, "What is the one thing that is standing in the way of what Jesus wants you to be?" Once they have answered that question, then we can together work on any or all of the other issues they face.

My God specializes in the impossible. You have no impossible situations that God cannot fix. The apostle Paul puts it this way: **"And my God shall supply all your need according to His riches in glory by Christ Jesus."** (Philippians 4:19 NKJV) God says it. I believe it. Anyone can believe it. That settles it for everyone. The question for me is a simple question. "How and where do I go from here?" I hear the answer. **"Follow me, and I will make you fishers of men."** (Mark 4:19) I am determined that I will follow Him to the best of my ability as a fisher of men. The Lord will have to open doors that will permit me to reach the gay community with love.

Living a Godly Life

How can I say that God sanctified me, and at the same time have written some of the things that I have shared with you? Answering that question could well be a life's work. I was saved in prison. I was baptized with the Holy Spirit in college. I have lived a life of service to God. I have walked in holiness with God and before all mankind. How? The how is about my conservative Evangelical Wesleyan Armenian viewpoint.

The Apostle Paul puts it this way. **"Work out your own salvation with fear and trembling; for it is God who is works in you both to will and to do for His good pleasure." (Philippians 2:12-13)** God worked in me until I was able to see what He saw, and I did not like it. I used foul language, I was angry on the inside, I failed at living for Him, and I could keep on going. After I became filled with the Holy Spirit, that all changed. I found that there was nothing between me and God. I have endeavored, with the help of the Holy Spirit to keep it that way, and I make sure that there is nothing between me and anyone else. I love them for Christ's sake, and I go because His loves compels me to love my neighbor by all that I have at my disposal. I practice my faith!

Jesus answered a Levitical lawyer's question: "Teacher what is the great commandment of the law" with these words? **"You shall love the Lord your God with all your heart, with all your soul, and with all your mind. And the second is like it. You shall love your neighbor as yourself." (Matthew 22:37-39 NKJV)** Once God's Holy Spirit works on your heart, then you are able to work out your salvation. God works in me, and He is working for my good.

I have read, researched, thought, and studied about how I know that God has worked in my life. I have prayed about the best way to express what I believe is reality in my life. Again, I want to express that this is the story of my life. It is about me. This is not a research paper. I have experienced in my life what I believe. God wants us to be like Him. How?

God wants to take what is on the inside of a person and cleanse it, and He wants to make that person able to live a Holy Life. As a Wesleyan-Armenian, I live a holy life for God. I have a problem. God forgives and forgets my sins that I have committed. (Jeremiah 31:34; Hebrews 10:17) God forgets. I don't forget. Satan causes the believer to be tempted and to remember. He is noted as the accuser of the (our) brethren. (Revelation 12:10) In simple words, "I remember my past because Satan keeps bringing it up." God has another plan. His Holy Spirit works in my heart and the Spirit helps changes my heart. I may not understand how it works. It just does!

I will use three separate scriptures to help give you have an understanding of what I mean. The first is the story of when the prophet Nathan confronted David about his sin with Bathsheba. He told the story of a rich man that had many sheep, but stole and killed the one sheep of his poor neighbor for his feast. David was an angry man as he listened. Nathan replied, "You are the man; and you killed her husband, Uriah the Hittite."David repented in sorrow. Read Psalm 51: especially these words. **"Have mercy upon me, O God ... Wash me thoroughly from my iniquity, and cleanse me from my sin." (Psalm 52:1-2 NKJV)** In this Psalm David not only wanted what he had done forgiven, he wanted a thorough work done in his life. The Apostle Paul in writing to the Thessalonica Church writes these words of blessing, **"Now may the God of peace Himself sanctify you completely; and may your whole spirit, soul and body be preserved blameless at the coming of our Lord Jesus Christ. He who calls you will also do it." (1Thessalonians 5:2-24 NKJV)** God wants us to be forgiven. He wants us to be cleansed throughout our entire being. He wants us to be perfect (mature) as he is perfect. **(Matthew 5:48 NKJV)** The writer of Hebrews in chapter thirteen has great pithy messages for the Jewish Believers. "Let brotherly love continue" (v. 1), "Remember the prisoners" (v. 3), "Jesus Christ the same yesterday, today and forever" (v.8), and, finally in benediction he writes, **"May the God of peace who brought up our Lord Jesus from the dead, that great shepherd of the sheep, through the blood of the everlasting covenant, make you complete in every good work to do His will, working in you what is well pleasing in His sight, through**

Jesus Christ, to whom be glory forever and ever. Amen." (Hebrews 13:20-21 NKJV)

God wants change as we live our life. He wants Christ to forgive our sins as we repent. He desires the Holy Spirit to clean up our lives. He calls us, out of a holy lifestyle, to serve him now and throughout eternity. I have accepted His challenges: the challenge to win my family and friends to him, the challenge to go wherever – to hospitals, to prisons, to homes, to anywhere and at any cost, and now I have accepted the challenge of going to the lesbian, gay, bisexual, and transgendered (LGBT). As I have researched, in the words of the Rev. John Wesley, "The world is my parish!" On nearly every continent and in every country on the planet, we hear of sexual problems such as broken homes, HIV and AIDS, and sin of every kind. I could keep expanding. God called me to live absolutely in all of my being for Him. With an Amen, I accept the challenge before me!

Section Two

Bible Study Guides

ON THE BIBLE STUDY GUIDES

I started my autobiography using a devotional guide format. I wanted to use a selection of Scripture, a written devotional thought, and close with an appropriate scripture, affirmation or prayer. However, this did not seem to provide the continuity that was needed. Superintendent Jeffrey P. Johnson suggested that I write to my son, Myke. This has been accomplished, and it has provided the continuous thought that was needed. The two together have intertwined with the story of my life and provided what was needed. I have kept the Bible study guides. This has provided a way to say things in a short and meaningful manner and at the same time to help those interested to work through some of the issues that I have faced over the years. Some of those are anger, aloneness, stubbornness, masturbation, dreams, and temptation. The one thing that will help you as you continue reading is to keep your Bible handy. I am not trying to push my faith onto anyone. I am a believer, and that is a part of my autobiography.

A Letter to Myke

The date of my conversion, November 18, 1952, marked a transition in my life. It is time to turn the corner and to get a glimpse of where God has led me in my life.

First, I want to make a disclaimer. I am not including what others think about me. I am sure that I could do so. However, I'll let you decide on your own whether I was an "unforgettable character or not. My Christian life goal has been to live as the most forgettable character you have ever known. Each person will have to decide that for themselves. This is my affirmation, "I have and will continue to write honestly."

As I transition and look towards the end, I sense a desire to pull the loose ends together and to bring focus to where I am heading. First, it has been heart wrenching as I have looked back at that which I have experienced. I have felt the agony I put Sandra and my parents through, and possibly what I have put all the members of my family through, including you. Tears have streamed down my face for them and for you. I have had to ask God for forgiveness anew, and He has granted that forgiveness. Every dark cloud has a silver lining. The dark thread that has coursed through my writing thus far is the thread of bisexuality.

I have heard recently, "But, you are a Christian now. You are not bisexual anymore." I am very aware of that. But Satan knows where to get a hold on me. I live constantly with who I was and who I am now, and I scream "Why?" until I realize that God is calling me to walk with Him into the LGBT community. First, I need to reveal to you the transitions that have gotten me to the place where I am going. I had to learn how to live a Christian life, how to transition to a civilian life, how to be academically prepared, how to maintain a celibate life, how to minister as a pastor, and lastly how I am to minister as a chaplain and pastor to the LGBT Community.

God does forgive acts of sin. However, He sanctifies us from our naturally sinful nature, and I have to define for you what I believe about orientation, predisposition, and learned behavior. As I close this cover letter, please remember that I am telling you about my life and not yours.

With all my love,

Dad

A Dream in the Night

"Too much activity gives you restless dreams; too many words make you a fool ... talk is cheap, like daydreams and other useless activities. Fear God instead." (Ecclesiastes 5:3, 7. NLT) **"For in the multitude of many words there is also vanity. But Fear God."** (Ecc. 5:7 NKJV).

There are just about 110 references to dreams in the Bible. Here, the word "activity" can be translated to mean concern, a typical subject of human dreams. Though they have little meaning, dreams often reflect natural anxieties and concerns. In verse seven, the line could be translated, "For many useless things and words [come] in an abundance of dreams."(NKJV)

I had a restless dream-filled evening last night. It was filled with chaos and time after time, in my dreams, I was on the verge of having homosexual contact with someone. I could see the man, but I did not know him. I knew it was a dream, but it was a dream almost bordering on reality. In a sexual sense, it could have been classified as a "wet dream." It was so real that my project for the next day was trying to understand why.

A spiritual glimpse at Acts 2:17, (NKJV) taken from the Book of Joel 2:28-32, may give us a couple of ideas worth considering. **"And it shall come to pass in the last days, says God, that I will pour out My Spirit on all flesh; ... your young men will see visions, your old men will dream dreams."** The word "dream" in the Old Testament has the idea not only to dream but also to cause to dream. In the New Testament, young men do not need to dream. They see visions, and in the vigor of their youth, they go for it. Meanwhile, old men envision in their sleep and have only dreams – they dream dreams.

I do not remember anything that would have triggered what happened last night in my dreams. I have no answer. This is what I did. During my personal time with God that morning, I told him about my night of dreams and my concern about them. I asked Him to not to permit it to happen again, and I further asked that His Holy Spirit would help me in that regard and that my search might help others to find a way to obtain help from God in every area of their lives.

The Book of Ecclesiastes concludes with these words, and my prayer is found in those words. **"Fear (worship) God and keep His commandments, for this is man's all. For, God will bring every work into judgment, including every secret thing, whether good or evil" (12:13-14 NKJV).** Amen!

A Delicate Subject (Masturbation)

"Then the Lord God said, 'It is not good for the man to be alone. I will make a helper who is just right for him.'" (Genesis 2:18 NLT)

I have searched the Word of God many times to find an answer to "A Delicate Subject". The subject before us is not usually talked about, especially in polite society. But, I have a feeling that nearly every person, male or female, at one time or another has wrestled with the problem. The subject is self-manipulation, more commonly known as masturbation. Masturbation is the "stimulation of manipulation of one's own genitals, especially to orgasm."[9]

The subject is seldom discussed even among those of the same sex. The general attitude is, "Others do it, but not me," and if you admit to practicing it, you are some kind of loony tune. I first had the experience when I was nine and a half years of age. I noted that when I was getting out of bed in the morning, my penis was stiff, and as I inspected the matter, it spit at me. It felt good. I never even thought of asking my parents about this phenomenon. There just appears to be some things that you do not ask or tell others. What about this?

Let us look at the above verse of Scripture, **"It is not good for man to be alone."** [These are the writer's thoughts, and I purposely have not done any research about what other opinions might be. This is my life story and my experience.] Will you picture with me?

God has made man in His own image. He has breathed into his nostrils the breath of life. God placed Adam over His creation in the Garden of Eden. I can only picture him as a strong man in the prime of life with all of the possibilities of procreation, and suddenly God gets on with business. **"I will make him a helper who is just right for him."** God did not want self-manipulation. He wanted man to be fulfilled in procreation with his wife.

[9] Random House Webster's College Dictionary. (2000). New York, NY: Random House.

In the Ten Commandments, God says, **"You shall not commit adultery."** He never said, "You shall not masturbate," and there are some who might reason that God made that omission purposely, knowing there might be times when an unmarried man would need to fulfill himself sexually. This may be especially true after the death of a spouse.

You may want to consider two things to help you make the right choice for yourself. First, Jesus said to the disciples in the 'Sermon on the Mount', **"Whoever looks at a woman to lust after her has already committed adultery with her in his heart."** This reminds us to be sure that we do not fantasize during the act of masturbation. Secondly, the Apostle Paul in Romans 14 writes about liberty and love, and how eating meat and drinking wine may affect our Christian relationships. In the midst of the discussion, the Apostle writes, **"Happy is he who does not condemn himself in what he approves."** (Romans 14:22 B NKJV) If there is self-condemnation, I would say, "Quit it and ask for forgiveness, and ask the Holy Spirit to help you where you cannot help yourself."

There is probably one piece of advice I could give to you. If you have no peace concerning the matter of self-manipulation, you need to go to God in prayer. He understands. He permitted you to be made just like you were made, whether man or woman. We find in the Epistle to the Philippians, **"Be anxious about nothing, but in everything by prayer and supplication, with thanksgiving, let your requests be made known to God; and the peace of God... will guard your hearts and minds through Christ Jesus."** (4:6-7)

Father, as we consider the matter of masturbation, will you help us through prayer and fasting to come up with your answer for our lives? The answer that will satisfy our needs as well as to glorify you! Amen!

Stubbornness

"For rebellion is as the sin of witchcraft, and stubbornness is as iniquity and idolatry. Because you have rejected the word of the Lord, He has rejected you (King Saul) from being king." (1 Samuel 15:23 NKJV)

The word "stubborn" means to turn away or backslide, to peck at, i.e. figuratively to dull or stun. [10] The word is used only in the Old Testament, and then only seven times. I must admit that I am stubborn and rebellious. Let me explain. God put it on my heart to write my biography shortly after November 1988. I have been side-stepping that issue ever since. This has happened for two reasons: time commitment and because of the content and the life that I have lived.

However, God has had enough of me. Briefly, I remember all of the reasons I gave for not accepting Him as my Savior. I had used the same arguments for not accepting His call to be a pastor. Now, the reasons are a little different, but virtually the same and God was not accepting them. An explanation is needed.

I went to the Ministers' Institute of the North East (MINE) at Willow Valley, Pennsylvania. Our new Bishop, David Roller, was there to challenge the pastors. He used an Old Testament Patriarch, Terah, (Genesis 11:31-32), in his message titled "Going Home" with a subtitle "Beyond These Walls." The Bishop posed such questions as: What am I leaving behind? What do I stop doing? Not enough money? How do I minister to broken people? Especially the last question was as relevant to octogenarians as to teenagers. I was forced to agree with the Bishop's statement, "The Church needs to determine to get on with the task that Jesus has called us to as a body of believers.

---

[10] Random House Webster's College Dictionary. (2000). New York, NY: Random House.

The other speaker for MINE 2008 was Dr. Reggie McNeal. He highlighted the fact that this is the first time the Church has had to deal with a six generational culture. He dealt with a Church that is program-driven or one that is geared for people development. While these two men of God and the issues facing the Church today were challenging me, God had another agenda for my life.

My take-away was my response to His insistence that I write. I want to be me. If I am to minister to the gay community, I need to be out of the closet. If I am to minister to the gay community, I cannot fly under false colors. I need to be able to contact people in the community who can help me. I am listing four scripture references that you can consider and that I need to work upon. (Hebrews 13:3; Luke 4:18; 1 Corinthians 6:9-11; and 1 Corinthians 10:13.) I felt as though God and the content of the conference were tearing me in two. At the end of MINE, I was broken and literally in tears. I know that the experiences I had on that occasion will forever change my life. I experienced what Jeremiah the Prophet experienced when he wrote,

"My eyes flow and do not cease, without interruption. Till the Lord from Heaven looks down and sees." *(Lamentations 3:49-50 NKJV) By God's mercy I will pursue the end of stubbornness.*

Temptation

"We do not have a High Priest who cannot sympathize with our weaknesses, but was in all points tempted as we are, yet without sin. Let us therefore come boldly to the throne of grace, that we may obtain mercy and find help in time of need." (Hebrews 4:15-16 NKJV) We need to take a look at Jesus. He was both God and man. I believe that we can conclude that if God's son could be tempted, then we as mere mortals can certainly be tempted.

Temptation is almost worse than sin, at least in my experience. I have been tempted in many ways. It is hard to imagine that our Lord Jesus Christ was ever tempted. Everyone has been tempted at one time or another. Addictions come in all shapes and sizes. The alcoholic is tempted with just one little drink. The bisexual person is tempted by revealing clothes and bulges in all the right/wrong places. The gambler is tempted with all of the different gambling devices available today. There's something for everyone.

A brief look at some scripture verses will help us see the problem a little more clearly. In the Lord's Prayer, we are taught to petition the Lord with these words: **"And do not lead us into temptation, but deliver us from the evil one."** (Matthew 6:13A) We also read that **"Jesus, being filled with the Holy Spirit, returned from the Jordan and was led by the Spirit into the wilderness being tempted forty days by the devil."** (Luke 4:1-2) Jesus was tempted by the devil in three different ways. He was tempted in his body **("Command this stone to become bread")**, He was tempted in the area of worship and the spiritual aspect of His life **("The devil ... showed Him all the Kingdoms of the World")**, and finally He was tempted with worldly power **("Throw yourself down from here")** (See Matthew 4:1-11). Jesus was tempted physically, spiritually and emotionally. He was tempted in His body, soul, and mind.

The word "tempted" or "tested" in the Greek contains the idea to explore, test, examine, prove, or attempt. According to the annotations in the New Spirit Filled Life Bible, "The word describes the testing of the believer's loyalty, strength, opinions, disposition, condition, faith, patience or character. The word 'tempted' determines which way one is going and what one is made of." (New Spirit Filled Life Bible, page 1820, at Revelation 2:10) The Apostle Paul puts it another way. **"No temptation has overtaken you except such is common to man; but God is faithful, who will not allow you to be tempted beyond what you are able, but with the temptation will also make a way of escape, that you may be able to bear it."** (1 Corinthians 10:13)

I can conclude two simple facts from the above. The purpose of temptation is to determine what I am made of and which way am I going. Also, I need to know that there is a way of escape. What is it? God will bind Satan, and He will send His angels to give us victory over the temptation, no matter what it might happen to be. It was true for Jesus and it will be true for us as well.

Strength to Resist Temptation

"Seeing then that we have a great High Priest who has passed through the heavens, Jesus the Son of God, let us hold fast our confession. For we do not have a High Priest who cannot sympathize with our weakness, but was in all points tempted as we are yet without sin. Let us therefore come boldly to the throne of grace, that we may obtain mercy and find grace to help in time of need." (Hebrews 4:14-16 NKJV)

I was asked this question recently by a friend: "How are you strong enough to resist temptation?" I knew that we both experienced a common temptation as individuals. How do I answer him? He asked the question because I have walked with God for 62 years in integrity, and He has only been a Christian for a short time. My first reaction was to answer, "Just say no." Be sure you do not watch pornography, and stay away from your temptation. Do not go where you know you will be tempted! I want to insert a personal note here. I made it a rule never to go into a restaurant and bar for about twelve years after I became a Christian. I knew that if I ever drank, I would not have the strength to say "No" to any temptation that came my way. Further, I did not want anyone that knew I was a Christian to wonder why I was in a restaurant that sold alcoholic beverages. Today it hardly matters, because there are only a few alcohol free restaurants or stores for that matter.

I asked my friend how he viewed me as a Christian being tempted. He responded positively. Then, I asked him how he would perceive me if I gave into temptation. He stated that he had no problem with it, and that he would still perceive me as a Christian. But, all this did not answer the question that he really was asking me. "How are you strong enough to resist temptation?" It appears to me that temptation is often worse on you than if you had actually committed sin. For me, the guilt associated with temptation is worse. You seem to savor it too much.

First, I accepted Christ as my Savior. I determined that I wanted nothing to tarnish that relationship. Therefore, I say a resounding "No," even if it is a little weak at times. Secondly, I use every means I have available to strengthen my relationship to the one who forgave my sins and loved me unconditionally. I read His word daily. I pray daily. I attend a Bible-believing Church. I attend all services that are meant to strengthen me in the Lord – Bible Study, worship, prayer meeting. Thirdly, I personally have made it a habit of my life to have personal and family devotions daily. Last, but not least, is that I serve Christ and the Church with all of my abilities. This is not all accomplished in one easy lesson. You work at it until it becomes habit.

However, how do I answer my friend's question from a practical Biblical standpoint?

Be sure of your salvation. There are many passages in God's word that can be used to lead a person to Christ. Psalm 24 is a classic and I John 1:1-10 and Ephesians 2:1-10 are great, but the one that really captures me at this moment is John 3:1-7. This last one I would like to highlight. Nicodemus came to Jesus my night. The interchange of dialogue between him and Jesus is electric. "Rabbi, we know that You are a teacher come from God, for no one can do these signs (miracles) that You do unless God is with Him." In verse three Jesus replies, "Unless you are born again, you cannot see the Kingdom of God." Nicodemus shoots back, "How can a man be born when he is old? Can He enter a second time into his Mother's womb and be born? Jesus replied, "Unless one is born of water and the Spirit, he cannot enter the kingdom of God." Jesus noted two things that could not happen unless they were born again. Individuals cannot see or enter the Kingdom of God. In verse seven, He reinforces His argument with Nicodemus, "Do not marvel that I said to you, 'You must be born again.'" Note that Jesus continues the exchange with one interruption from His night visitor: "How can these things be?" Jesus continues through verse 21. The Golden text of the Bible, John 3:16, very succinctly says it very forcefully, "For God so loved the world that he gave His only begotten Son, that whoever believes in Him should not perish but have everlasting life." I immerse myself in these passages and praise God for my salvation.

1. **Read God's Word.** I try to reinforce my salvation by reading His word. Isaiah 55:11 says it very clearly: "So shall My word be that comes out of My mouth; it shall not return to Me void, but it shall accomplish what I please, and it shall prosper in the thing for which I sent it." (NKJV) I put it this way: get into God's word, and permit God's word to get into you. Psalm 119, the longest chapter in the Bible says it very well in 176 verses. I put the Word of God into practice in my life.

2. **Next, take time to pray.** Jesus' disciples asked Him to teach them to pray, and He gave them the Lord's Prayer. It can be found in Luke 11:1-13 and Matthew 6:5-15. Read until you understand, and then practice what you have learned. An old songwriter put it this way: "Take time to pray, speak oft with the Lord." A great hymn, by Albert Simpson Reitz, says it all. "Teach Me to Pray." The first night that I became a Christian, I prayed, "Lord, teach me to pray!" I did not know how to pray. Can you imagine what happened about six months later, when that hymn was one of the songs that were sung in our worship service where I was attending? Tears of joy poured down my face.

3. **Work on escaping your particular temptation.** You need to know that Jesus experienced temptation. "For we do not have a High Priest who cannot sympathize with our weaknesses, but was in all points tempted as we are, yet without sin." (Hebrews 4:15 NKJV) Another great verse is I Corinthians 10:13, (NKJV) "No temptation has over taken you such as is common to man; but God is faithful, who will not allow you to be tempted beyond what you are able, but with the temptation will also make the way of escape that you may be able to endure it." Find it, read it, memorize it, and experience the fact that your Savior is there to help you.

4. Serve the Lord by putting into practice what you have learned.
Read, pray, rely on Jesus when you are tempted, and lastly serve your
Master! Jesus gave the great commission to His disciples in Matthew
28:18-20. Read it carefully. Put it into practice. That is what I have
been doing as I answer my friend's question. Friends, I pray that that
you will experience what you find in John 15:12-17.

> [12] This is My commandment, that you love one
> another as I have loved you. [13] Greater love has
> no one than this, than to lay down one's life for
> his friends. [14] You are My friends if you do
> whatever I command you. [15] No longer do I call
> you servants, for a servant does not know what
> his master is doing; but I have called you
> friends, for all things that I heard from My
> Father I have made known to you. [16] You did
> not choose Me, but I chose you and appointed
> you that you should go and bear fruit,
> and *that* your fruit should remain, that
> whatever you ask the Father in My name He
> may give you. [17] These things I command you,
> that you love one another.

It is worth all the work that you will put into it. It will not be easy, but
the best things in life are never easy. Simply put, just say "No," and
mean it, because you are going to have to work at being the greatest
Christian that you can be with Jesus' help. Amen!

Alone

There are eight Hebrew words for "alone" in the Old Testament used in 65 different references. There are 13 Greek words use in 37 instances in the New Testament. I found that there are 102 references to "alone" in the entire Bible. The word means separation, solitude, alone, and alone by themselves. It is used in reference to things as well as to people. I do not like being alone. I have cried out many times, "I want to be me!" when I have been alone.

I spent a Christmas and a New Year in Boston visiting Scully's Square. I was surrounded by many people, but I was lonely. I had the same experience in Greenwich Village, New York City. I have felt the same on Market Street in San Francisco, and in the French Quarter in New Orleans during Mardi Gras. There is one thing I have noted as I have researched the LGBT community. Many express this same feeling of aloneness. I believe that the feeling of aloneness can come from coming out to our families and subsequently immersing ourselves in the gay lifestyle. The two are not in the same ballpark by any means.

I want to point you to an example of one man who never experienced the feeling of aloneness. He simply tells us that He and the Father are one. That person is the Son of God. Jesus was in Jerusalem one morning, and as He was teaching in the Temple, the Scribes and Pharisees brought a woman to Him who was caught in the very act of adultery. They asked Him if they should stone her. He wrote in the sand, and He rose up to tell them, "He who is without sin among you, let him throw a stone at her first." They left without casting a stone, from the oldest to the last. Jesus found himself alone with the woman, and He addressed her, "Woman, where are those accusers of yours? Has no one condemned you?"

"No one, Lord."

Jesus said to her, "Neither do I condemn you, go and sin no more." (John 8:9 -11 NKJV)

Jesus reaffirmed His judgment in verses 16 and 29 of the same chapter. Listen: "My judgment is true; for I am not alone, but I am with the Father who sent me. And, He who sent Me is with Me. The Father has not left me alone, for I always do those things that please Him." Jesus wants to say the same thing to you. "Neither do I condemn you. Go and sin no more." I am sure as we give our lives over to his wonderful grace, we will experience in our life and in the lives of those around us what happened in the verse 30: "Many believed in Him."

Jesus desires to say to you the words that He spoke to those that believed Him, **"If you abide in My word, you are My disciples indeed. And you shall know the truth, and the truth shall make you free." (John 8:31-32)** I say, "It is true and it works. It has worked in my life." That incessant feeling of aloneness is not there. Amen!

Anger

Ephesians 4:25 - 5:2 (NKJV)

The Apostle Paul is talking to the church at Ephesus. In these hortatory sentences, he is not chastising them, but rather encouraging them. These sentences sound somewhat like the Ten Commandments. But, Paul is telling them how to live their lives. The word "Let" seems to be key to me. **"Let each one speak the truth in love; be angry and sin not, let not the sun down on your wrath; let him who stole steal no longer, let him labor; let no corrupt words proceed out of your mouth; let no corrupt communication proceed out of your mouth ... do not grieve the Holy Spirit; and be imitators of God and walk in love."** Verse 32 provides this word of encouragement: **"Be kind to one another, tender hearted, forgiving one another, even as God in Christ forgave you."**

My wife June had a good old tiff early in our marriage, and we did not talk with each other for three days. We slept back to back. When we got over our anger, we decided that we would never allow that to happen again. If we got upset with each other, we always settled it with a kiss before going to bed. It worked. Myke asked me one time, "Dad why do you get so angry sometimes?" I was not able to answer him, because I never had figured it out. I prayed about it and I came up with this answer. I was angry because of my previous lifestyle. I was not comfortable with having a gay orientation. Now, what do you do? That issue had to be resolved. I came across this passage in Colossians 3:12-16. It has to do with the character of the new man. In verse 13, these words stuck out at me, **"Even as Christ forgave you, so you also must do."** Christ forgave me for the acts of sin I had committed. However, I had carried around self guilt and I had not forgiven myself.

I looked into the mirror of my life, the inside of me, and I did not like what I saw. So I prayed, "I do not like what I have been or what I see. However, I forgive myself for the sin I have committed, and by faith I ask that your Holy Spirit will cleanse my heart from that over which I have no control."

Father, I ask that whoever reads or studies these words about anger will be able to look into their hearts and be able to forgive themselves for who they are without Christ, and that the Holy Spirit will cleanse their hearts by their faith in Jesus their Savior. Amen!

Suicide

Suicide is not an option in any situation. The preacher, King Solomon, wrote the book of Ecclesiastes. He begins with "Vanity of vanities, all is vanity." The Preacher called the ecclesia (the church) together to consider how they toil "under the sun." (1:1-3 NKJV) He ends the book with these words of wisdom after trying everything "under the sun": **"Fear God and obey His commandments, for this is everyone's duty."** (12:13 NLT) In between, he tries to **"Seek and search out by wisdom concerning all that is done under Heaven."** (1:13) I want to lift one word out of this book. That word is death, or more specifically, suicide. Essentially, God determines the day of our death. Read with me this one verse, **"No one has power over the spirit to retain the spirit, and no one has power over the day of death. There is no release from that war, and wickedness will not deliver those who have given it."** (8:8 NKJV)

I have had to deal with suicide in two different times in my life as a minister of the gospel. On two occasions, I have fought the battle personally. On one occasion, my marriage was not going well. I considered every avenue I could think of that would make escape possible without hurting others in the family. I considered driving or jumping in the front of an eighteen wheeler going about sixty or seventy miles an hour. I thought of getting one of my guns and ending life that way. But, what if I lived? I considered jumping off of a railroad bridge about 125 feet up. Again, what would that do to the ones I loved? I prayed and discarded all those options. About two years later, I was in the breakfast nook when my wife, son, and I had had a good old battle. I realized that if I took one step away from the window, nothing would have stopped me from ending my life. I made the decision to get counseling. I have never been plagued with that scenario again.

I have been called to officiate over a death that was by the individual's own decision. It is hard to minister to those left behind. The questions never seem to get answered. The irony was that in two weeks, he would have known that he was to have a baby son. I often wonder what his decision would have been then. His parents are helping the mother to raise his child.

This one verse gives us examples of other things that man cannot control or predict:

1. Man cannot force the spirit to stay in his body, keeping his body alive when it is time to die.
2. He cannot postpone death. (Though, he can hasten it.)
3. He cannot avoid service in time of war.
4. He cannot use wickedness to save himself, for it ensnares him.

This comment I feel is needed, because the culture in which we live is forcing mankind to consider the issue of suicide. I see it in the cases of military personnel coming home from military action. Good men can't seem to adjust, and their families are left with the guilt. I have seen it with sexual offenders. Society won't accept them. There may be occasions when the Church is unable to minister to their needs.

My advice is simple. Find yourself a counselor that you can trust. The best would be a spiritual counselor. At times of crisis, we need to bring our life together spiritually as well as physically. Prior to being sick last year, I had a friend that was a sexual offender. I met with him every Saturday afternoon for nearly a year. I would take him shopping. I would have a lunch with him. I would give him counsel and conclude the afternoon with prayer. It was the only thing that kept him from suicide. He pushed my buttons on several occasions concerning it. You may have to bring someone else alongside to help in the ministry. Friends of his and mine came alongside and we were able to get him into a home that could give him the stability he needed. Spiritual counseling works.

Please note, for those that are thinking of helping someone or of having someone help you, I have tried to include suggestions that should help you create or find an effective ministry. I have provided Biblical Study Guides that can be of help in different situations. I have included two books in my 'Selected Bibliography' that likewise may help as you counsel. These are <u>Competent to Counsel,</u> by Jay E. Adams, and <u>Reclaiming Surrendered Ground,</u> by Jim Logan. Finally, for the LGBT community, I would urge you to find a copy of <u>Sabbatical Journey,</u> by Henri J. M. Nouwen. In the diary he kept during sabbatical, he makes several references to ministry in the gay community.

Father, I ask that you will use the above to help those who feel there is no hope or that they have nothing to live for. Jesus, I pray that your grace may prevail in the lives of those who feel they have reached the end. Holy Spirit, I intercede for those who need you to bring them to a place where they can accept salvation in Christ our Lord and do not consider ending their life. Amen!

Patience, Faith, and Prayer

Profiting from Trials

"My brethren, count it all joy when you fall into various trials, knowing that the testing of your faith produces patience. But let patience have its perfect work, that you may be perfect and complete, lacking nothing. If any of you lacks wisdom, let him ask of God, who gives to all liberally and without reproach, and it will be given to him. But let him ask in faith, with no doubting." (James 1:2-6 New King James Version (NKJV))

The above topics were to be the last of the Bible Study Guides. But, they seemed to fit together, especially in the light of this selection from James. May we look at the first one? Patience is from a Greek word *(upomona)* meaning, patience, endurance, perseverance, or steadfastness. That one word is used for each of the applications. May I reword a part of the above? **"The testing of your faith produces endurance. You let patience have its perfect work, that you may be perfect and complete."** We have the same passage in The New International Version (NIV) translated, **"The testing of your faith develops perseverance. Perseverance must finish its work so that you may be mature and complete."**

God used this particular portion of His Word to quiet my heart as my third wife, Violet, and I were deciding to get married. Remember I had been divorced. She had no misgivings; but, I did. As we were having devotions, I was reading the above and Jesus brought peace into my heart. As I write, He probably gave it to me because I was a very impatient man. I wanted something done and done now! I could not stand a slow car in front of me. Now, I can slow down and smell the roses. Well, almost. The man of God must learn to be patient. This is true no matter how you have lived your life. Three brief verses come to mind:

"But the fruit of the Spirit is love, joy, peace, longsuffering (patience), kindness, goodness, faithfulness, gentleness, self-control. Against such there is no law." (Galatians 5:22-23 NKJV). The Apostle Paul in the "Great Love Chapter" of the Bible writes these simple words, **"Love is patient and it is kind."** (1 Corinthians 13:4-8 NIV) Again, in Paul's epistle to the Romans, he encourages the church to behave like Christians with these words, **"Rejoicing in hope, patient in tribulation, continuing steadfast in prayer."** (Romans 12:12 NKJV). Our society needs these verses at work in our lives. Every member of society needs to experience being long-suffering and kind, that love is patient and kind, and above all, patient in tribulation. This only comes about through faith and prayer.

"The testing of your faith produces patience." We must go all the way back to the Old Testament's Prophet Habakkuk for faith. Habakkuk asked God, "Why you are using the Chaldean nation, a nation worse than Judah and Jerusalem to punish your people?" God answered with these words: **"Behold the proud, his soul is not upright in him; but the just shall live by his faith."** (Habakkuk 2:4 NKJV) The Apostle Paul later uses the last half of this verse as he writes to the churches at Rome, at Galatia, and to the Hebrews. **"Now the just man will live by faith."** (Romans 1:17 - translated from the Greek) Later in his epistle to the Galatians in contrasting the law as opposed to faith, he writes **"The just shall live by faith."** (Galatians 3:11 NKJV) The writer of Hebrews writes, **"And He (Christ) who is coming will come and will not tarry. [But,] now the just shall live by faith."** (Hebrews 10:38 NKJV) The writer, from this point on, slips into the 'great chapter on faith.' He immediately writes **"Now faith is the substance of things hoped for, the evidence of things not seen."** (Hebrews 11:1 NKJV) And, we find listed in this great chapter about thirty people and circumstances that point to the power of faith.

May I summarize with a few brief words from G. Campbell Morgan with regards to the above? "In Habakkuk, the contrast is between being the "puffed up" and the 'just.' In Romans, God has provided righteousness for the ungodly. In Galatians, the law is a tutor to bring us to Christ. It is a great doctrine (teaching) of liberty from the law. In Hebrews, faith was the condition for the Old Testament law; and, so it is the same condition of the New Covenant in Christ." [11]

Such great faith leads us to the last word, "prayer". James 5:11-18 is one of the greatest lessons on prayer to be found in God's word. This passage opens and closes with two great men of God – Job and Elijah -- as illustrations. **"We count them blessed who endure (have patience). You have heard of the perseverance (patience) of Job and seen the end intended by the Lord – that the lord is very compassionate and merciful."** (V. 11) Seven times we read the words "pray" or "prayer". Once, we are encouraged to sing Psalms. **"To those who suffer, the writer addressed words full of tender comfort. He called them to patience. All that is said at the beginning of the letter concerning the value of trial in life is taken for granted remembering that God is working through all these processes toward bringing the fruit to maturity and ripeness, it is necessary that His people have patience."** Read carefully and be sure and answer the questions you find, as far as you are able to do so.

Would you please pray with me?

Father, we come to you asking for the enduring patience that only you can bring into our lives. We give thanks that through faith we can come to the reality of knowing "The just shall live by faith" in the Lord Jesus Christ throughout eternity. We thank you for the great gift of prayer that leads through faith to patient endurance. We thank you for the gift of the Holy Spirit that makes it all possible. Our Prayer is In the Name of the Father, the Son and the Holy Spirit. Amen.

---

[11] G. Campbell Morgan. An Exposition of the Whole Bible; Fleming H. Revell Company, Westwood, NJ, 1949.

Section Three

Appendices and Manuals

APPENDICES AND MANUALS

I have added to my autobiography this section for the primary purpose of helping myself and others to have guidelines for speaking engagements, one-on-one sessions, and for counseling. The appendices are a real part of the autobiography, but they are not essential to the story line. They furnish guidelines for ministry to others that are in or out of the gay community. Thus, we have an autobiography, Bible Study Guides, and a brief manual that should help those interested in setting up a ministry. The appendices include:

1. A Letter to Myke
2. Men of Integrity
3. A Letter to Minta
4. A Letter to Family and Friends
5. A Jubilee of Thanksgiving
6. Murder on the Nile
7. Questions and Answers
8. Plans of Salvation

Manual I – The Church Reaches Out

Manual II – Rehabilitation and Transformation

Manual III – Pastoral Guidelines

Recommended Readings

This is not an exhaustive list. It provides food for thought and discussion. The reader will have to formulate his or her own guidelines depending on their particular circumstances and audience.

Appendix One

A Letter to Myke

Dear Myke,

It has been my pleasure to share my life with you. It made me see myself in a complete new way. Usually, I compartmentalize everything. This has made me look at all the pieces. I have not liked what I realized has been true.

I have shared with you my early life, school, navy life, the story of four wives, of blended families, the church and the many ministries in which I have been involved, and the realization that, though I do not like being alone, I have been a loner at many times in different capacities. I am sure that you have experienced that aloneness as well. As you read, I want you to feel free to comment and please do not hesitate to make criticisms or ask questions. I want to be able to answer them from my prospective honestly and clearly in order that you will not feel left out of the equation. I have never had anyone that I was able to pursue a conversation with. You do. You have your Father.

Myke, I have worked hard on this project, and out of it has come a love for you and the ministry God has called me to, though that is hard to explain. Myke, it is called "Love." Thanks for that experience.

LOVE,

Dad

Appendix Two

"Men of Integrity," a Men's Breakfast Address

I want to begin this with a Samson-like riddle. "My eight children have six mothers and five fathers." May I explain? My first wife (Marian Elisabeth Bradt) and I had one daughter, Sandra Elaine, on August 30, 1946, at 12:15 P.M. Her mother passed away just eight hours later. I was married on my 21st birthday to Valerie Lee Camira ^ and was divorced June 16, 1948. I married Violet Martha Marville on July 7, 1956 at 1:00 P.M. in Camden, New Jersey. We had three children: William. Jr. on April 16, 1957; David Paul on October 17, 1959; and Rebekah Sue on April 17, 1963. While we were raising them, Stephan Sharpe^ of Allegany lived at our house almost continually until he became like a foster child. After Violet's death on May 8, 1979, I was married to M. June V. Smith Taylor on August 1, 1981. She had two children, Patricia Ann born January 4, 1949, and an adopted daughter, Sherry Lee. Her birthday is January 25, 1952. After our marriage, June and I adopted her oldest grandson, Michael Patrick Tice (Patricia's Son), on January 27, 1983. His birthday is November 20, 1969. My eight children have six mothers and five fathers.

My life verse is Hebrews 13:3. God gave me this verse early in my Christian life. **"Remember them that are in bonds, as bound with them; and them which suffer adversity, as being yourself also in the body."** (KJV)

I would like to read St. Luke 4:16-21. And, I would like to note that Jesus said, **"Today this scripture is fulfilled in your hearing."** *(NKJV)* And, I want to read another passage; and this is where my witness really starts.

"Do you not know that the unrighteous will not inherit the kingdom of God? Do not be deceived. Neither fornicators, nor homosexual, nor sodomites, nor thieves, nor covetous, nor drunkards, nor revilers, nor extortioners, will inheritthe kingdom of God. And such were some of you. But you were washed, but you were sanctified. , but you were justified in the name of the Lord Jesus and by the Spirit of our God." (1 Corinthians 6:9-11 NKJV)

By the time I was twenty-six years of age that Scripture was fulfilled in my life leaving nothing out. I want you to note three words: washed, sanctified, justified. When you read in Scripture "washed", you are really saying, "My sins have been forgiven." And, when you say "sanctified" you are saying, "My heart has been completely cleansed of all sin by the Word of God and the Holy Spirit." Finally, when you come to "justified", God says you stand in the presence of God entirely righteous. It is like all the sin in my life was forgiven, I was sanctified, and made righteous before God as though it never even happened. In the past two years, God has given me a verse that I believe was for occasions like this.

"But those who wait on the Lord Shall renew their strength. They shall mount up with wings like eagles. They shall run and not be weary. They shall walk and not faint." (Isaiah 40:31 NKJV)

One more emphasis: I would like to mention God's prevenient grace, the carnal nature of man, and the call of God on a man's life. First, I can look back on my life, and there are more times than I can remember of that the grace that goes before was a part of my life. Even being kicked out of the Navy on December 22, 1952 was a part of that Grace. Secondly, there is the carnal nature of man, that sinful nature that we are all born with. My personal opinion is that all of those items mentioned in 1 Corinthians 6:9-11 are a part of that nature. But, the Holy Spirit can come into your heart and life and completely cleanse your heart of all sin. Therefore, I can believe that I was born with a life-style that was not natural. But, praise God, He can wash your heart as white as snow. Lastly, there is the call of God on my life. I tried to tell God on numerous occasions that he did not want me to be a pastor or to be in the ministry.

It went like this. I have been divorced. I have drank. I have smoked. I have had sex in many ways. The list could keep going on. God would not listen to me.

In May of 1953, in the Wesleyan Methodist Church in Bradford, Pennsylvania, we had a series of missionary speakers under the leadership of Pastor Price P. Stark. The speaker on that night was a Baptist missionary to Cuba. I have no idea what his name was, but God was speaking to my heart. He had a great message. My problem is that I do not remember a single word he said. As, I was leaving my pew and preparing to shake his hand and tell him how much I appreciated him, this is the real message that he preached that night to me as he shook my hand, he said, "Mr. I have never seen such a sour-lemony, pickled-faced puss in all of my life. If I were you, I would do something about it." Afterwards, I went out on the porch of the Church and looked up at the moon. In the midst of my reflection, I made this affirmation. "If that is what it means to say 'No' to God, then, I am going to say 'Yes'." And ever since, I have been saying, "Yes".

This later addition to my witness was added on August 16, 2003, as I was thinking about death, who I am, what I have been, and a myriad of other things. I realized something "All Fear is Gone". Two great hymns express this fact, "All for Jesus" and "Because He Lives". "All Fear is Gone," combined with the text below causes me to sing and to praise God with a resounding, "Thank You Jesus!"

"And such were some of you: but you are washed, but you are sanctified, but you are justified in the name of the Lord Jesus, and by the Spirit of our God." (1 Corinthians 6:11 NJKV) Amen.

Appendix Three

A Letter to Minta

I wrote this letter to Minta after she had received an article from me about an election dealing with the same-sex marriage issue. She let me know that she did not appreciate the article in no uncertain terms. I responded to her with this letter.

June 29, 2008

Dear Minta,

I want to thank you for the reply to my forwarded email. I sent it to my immediate family members. My thought was that they can either delete it or contact the executive chamber to either oppose it or give approval. I did not think about either you or Myke.

I know that I have a gay son and I love him very much. Also, I love his siblings, my grandchildren, as well. I pray for each of you every day. I did not anticipate muddying the waters by sending the email. I telephoned the executive chamber and voiced my opinion and forwarded it to those I love and care about.

In regards to religious emails, I seldom send them. If I do, I send them to those that I think would appreciate them. I guess the best thing I can say is that I screen them and if they are not appropriate I do not send them. I did not know that you did not want to receive them. For me, it is one way to let you know that I am here and that I care. Please feel free to give direction. Otherwise I will continue my current practice.

I talked with your mother last evening after receiving your reply. I am sorry to hear that you are not feeling well. I will be praying for you. Minta, I can only speak for myself, not for my family. I know that things have been said in the past that I did not agree with, and I still do not agree with them. I thank you for the respect that you have shown me. I believe that I have returned that respect. If not, I ask you to please forgive me. You, Myke, and Matt are always welcome in my home, and you will continue to be.

On June 19th, I went to have lunch with Myke. He took me out to dinner for Father's Day. After lunch, I shared with him the first few pages of my biography. I am not sure that you know that until I was 26 that I was bi-sexual. I was more on the gay side than the other. I have continually shown my support for Myke and I will continue to do so. During the times that I have been married, I have been faithful to that relationship, except for my second wife. In that case, we were both messing around.

My goal in writing my biography is not to "bash" anyone. My goal is to reveal how God has worked in my life and thus give encouragement to others and to help them to know that God loves them. After Myke had finished reading what I had written, he noted that I could be a little more descriptive and colorful and offered some suggestions. Also, he offered to make the jacket for the book. My goal is to have the first draft done by Christmas. Just a note, I know that my children and some of my grandchildren know that I was kicked out of the Navy on December 22, 1952 for being homosexual. I had accepted Jesus as my Savior on November 18th, 1952, and I have walked with Him ever since. My relationship with Jesus colors everything that I do in the church as well as in my family, and you are a part of that family. Minta, I would like you to reply to what I have written. Where I have hurt you, I simply ask your forgiveness. I did not do it maliciously, please believe me. I respect each one of you too much to do that.

I do not know what you mean by your lifestyle. Please share with me if you care to do so. If I have erred, it is in the fact that I have not been open about my past. I feel that this is what God wants me to rectify. I want you to know it is not easy to be out of the closet and out in the open at the age of 81, especially to those that you love, even when God the Father is urging you to do so.

Yours in love,

Dad

Appendix Four

A Letter to Family and Friends

Dear family and friends,

Some of you may know that I have been working on my autobiography. This letter is a part of the project. God has been after me for over 25 years to do it. Likewise, a couple of my grandkids have held me accountable. Until I was 26, I lived a life that I do not like to think or talk about. However, I have lived a life of integrity before God for 62 years. My goal, as I began to live my life for Jesus, was simply this: When I was in High School I was required to read "The Reader's Digest" as a part of my class assignment in English, and I was tested upon it. In those days, they always had a story in the back of it that told a story under this by-line – "The Most Unforgettable Character I Ever Met." I determined that I wanted to be that kind of man and that kind of Christian.

I do not know whether I have ever obtained that goal. One other goal that I set for myself as I began to preach was that I wanted to be a Bishop of the Church. That never happened – the statute of limitations ran out on me and I became too old. I do not want time to run out on this current phase of my life. Last August 1, 2009, I was reading as my devotional for the morning, "Our Daily Bread". The title was "Biography of God." The first half of the devotional applies to what I am requesting from you, "What do others say about you?"

I want to include some of your thoughts in my biography. If you feel led to reply, and my prayer is that you will, please let me know if you want your name included. I want to be sensitive in regards to you. You may email me, if you desire, rather than write me. My biography is not something that I have wanted to do. God has not given me any rest over the last several years. As in all of my altercations with my wonderful Savior, I am losing the battle. But, there is a peace in my heart because I have lost that battle. Please feel free to talk with me. It has not been easy to be out of the closet about my past life. But, as I have had occasion to reveal my life to others, and as I have become obedient to Him, it has given me a freedom that I had not known previously.

In the culture in which we are a part, I can sense the need for such a biography. God has laid a real burden on my heart for the gay community. How can they be reached for Him? Do you have any suggestions? As I write this, I am well aware that I am the father of some of you, brother of others, uncle to others, and a friend to many of you. Tears well up in my eyes as I bare my heart to you. I know what I am asking of you, and I equally know what God is asking of me. Please be in prayer as I try to obey His will for my life.

Yours in His Love,

Dad

Appendix Five

A Jubilee of Thanksgiving

I desire to take this occasion to thank my family and my friends of Wyoming County and Western New York for the opportunity of having served in the Gospel Ministry for the past 60 years. I am deeply humbled as I bow in a prayer of Thanksgiving and adoration to my Savior and Lord, Jesus Christ, and praise Him for this ministry. Equally, I am overwhelmed by the love and support many of you have given me during those years of ministry. There are people too numerous to mention that have enriched my life and that of my family with gifts, prayers, and in many other ways. I recall baptisms, weddings, funerals, hospital visits, jail visits, and other areas that have caused tears of gratitude to slide down my cheek.

I would like to list the churches and other areas of Ministry that have been a significant part of my life over the last 60 Years. It all began June 13, 1954.

Lamont Community Church, Castile, NY	1954 -- 1955
Marshall Community Church, Belfast, NY	Summer Supply 1956
The Federated Church, Ischua, NY	1957 -- 1958
Free Methodist Church, East Randolph, NY	1961 -- 1962
Genesee Conference FMC, Camping Ministry	1962 -- 1989
Christian, Missionary & Alliance Salamanca, NY (Interim Pastor)	Nov. 1964 - June 1965
Free Methodist Church, Olean, NY	1965 -- 1972
Coleman Memorial Free Meth. Church, Perry	1972 -- 1979
Free Methodist Church, Dansville, NY	1979 -- 1985
Coleman Memorial FMC, Perry, NY	1985 -- 1991

Wyoming County Jail Ministry, (Chaplain)	1974 -- 1979
Livingston County Jail Ministry, (Counseling)	1979 -- 1985
Wyoming County Jail Ministry, (Chaplain) 2013	1985 -- 2003, 2010-
Retirement from Active Ministry	1991 --
Valley Chapel FMC, Warsaw, NY	2002 -- Dec, 2012
Chaplain to the Gay Community	July 11, 2011 --
Ransomville FMC, Ransomville, NY	Jan. 2013 --

May the Lord richly bless each of you who have given me the blessed opportunity to serve the Lord Jesus and Western New York in the Gospel Ministry for nearly six decades.

Appendix Six

Murder on the Nile
A Sermon given by my son, Bill Jr.

September 28-29, 2013
Lesson: Exodus 2:11-25

Today I want to look at someone who I believe many of us know. I want to talk about his journey. Someone who seemed destined to end up on the ash heap of history. But, as is often the case, God had very different plans for life. His name is Moses and his story begins in Exodus 2. As you are turning to that text, let me set the context, because the context is incredibly important. The children of Israel had moved down from the land of Canaan to Egypt. They came to Egypt because of a famine that had taken place in Canaan and in Egypt as well. You may remember that Joseph, who was one of Jacob's sons who had been in Canaan, but who had been sold by his brothers into slavery, has now risen to leadership in Egypt. He helped the Egyptians to navigate through and prepare for the famine.

So in essence, the children of Israel follow the food down to Egypt, and, when the famine is over, they end up staying. They like Egypt – it is a good place to live. They settle down and they begin have lots and lots of babies. Lots of babies. Their numbers begin to grow exponentially. This growth begins to cause some angst and some concern among the leadership of Egypt. They think that the Israelites are getting too big, too powerful, and too influential. So they placed slave masters over the Israelites and forced them to become slave laborers.

We are told in Exodus 1 that they "Worked them ruthlessly." So all of a sudden, life that has been just gets turned on its heels. The Israelites, even under this oppression, continue to grow. So, Pharaoh puts out an edict. Basically, he orders genocide. He orders the Hebrew midwives to kill the male Hebrew babies as they are being born.

Please note verses Exodus 1:15-17.

"Then the king of Egypt spoke to the Hebrew midwives, of whom the name of one was Shiphrah and the name of the other Puah; and he said, 'When you do the duties of a midwife for the Hebrew women, and see them on the birth stools, if it is a son, then you shall kill him; but if it is a daughter, then she shall live.' But the midwives feared God, and did not do as the king of Egypt commanded them, but saved the male children alive."

But, the midwives practice what we would call "civil disobedience," and they refused to do what Pharaoh said. When they were asked why, basically they lied. They feared God. They said, "The Hebrew women are not like the Egyptian women." They just pop them out. They come out even before we get there!

Then Pharaoh issues an even more hideous edict! He orders that every Hebrew boy is to be thrown into the Nile River. That command leads to not just civil disobedience on the part of the midwives. It leads to vast civil disobedience on the part of many of the Israelites, including one very special mom who we read about in Exodus 2:1-4. This is where the story of Moses begins.

She puts him in the river knowing that as he floats downstream he is going to be found by some of the people in Pharaoh's court who bathed in the river. That's exactly what happened. One of Pharaoh's daughters came to bathe and saw the basket, and she saw that it was one of the Hebrew children, one of the boys, who was supposed to be killed. Her heart is broken, and she has compassion for this little boy.

Now, this is where we see how resourceful this little baby's mom really is. When Moses' sister sees that Pharaoh's daughter has found the baby, she approaches Pharaoh's daughter and asks her if she would like help in finding a Hebrew wet nurse who could nurse the baby. Pharaoh's daughter knew the dynamics of what was going on. She said, "Yes." This is what we are told in Exodus 2:1-10. [Read]

So, we see not only how smart and how resourceful this mom is. Not only does this mom get to nurse her own son, who feared of him being killed in the genocide that is going on. She gets paid by Pharaoh's daughter to take care of her own son. Maybe this is where we should end today: Mom's should get paid. Let's close with prayer. No!

When Moses gets to the age of about five or eight, the typical time this would have happened, Moses goes to Pharaoh's house. There, Moses is invited into the corridors of power. There, Moses gets access to a world class education. He gets access to incredible resources – things that he would never have access to as a member of an oppressed people group.

He is perfectly positioned to help his people in the midst of their oppression, having been able to spend his first five or six years with his biological mom in the Hebrew context to understand the Hebrew culture and get a sense of his identity. Then later, being raised as a young Prince in Pharaoh's house gives him the training, the expertise, and the resources to be a great leader.

He is perfectly positioned it seems for what God has intended Moses to do. But now, when he is all grown up, he makes the biggest mistake of his life. He sees an Egyptian beating a Hebrew man and instead of just intervening and stopping the act from taking place, though he certainly would have the authority that comes from being in that position, he loses his temper, goes into this fit of rage and ends up killing the Egyptian.

Moses then tries to cover the whole thing up by burying the Egyptian in a shallow sandy grave. It sounds just like an episode of "The Sopranos." He is hoping no one is going to find out, but they do find out, and the next day he realizes that not just a few people found out, but a lot of people have found out. Now Moses has a knot in the pit of his stomach that a lot of people could probably identify with. It's the feeling we get when we know that we have been caught, and we know there are going to be consequences. We see our life in some respect flashing before our eyes. That's what Moses is going through. He is overcome with fear, and his fear is not just in his consequences of what he has done; his fear is that maybe his whole life is going to be defined by this. His life defined by the worst thing that he has ever done – defined by his failure.

Then, things just go from bad to worse. When Pharaoh finds to what has happened, he tries to have Moses killed. Moses goes on the run and he ends up in a place called Median. Basically, it is in the middle of the desert. It is nowhere! Yikes. He ends up sitting by a well in the middle of the desert, and that is where he spends the next forty years of his life. He spends those years tending sheep in the middle of nowhere.

Physically separated from his biological family, rejected by his adoptive family, he is a man who is without a country, a man without a nation, and quite literally in the prison of exile. Forty years go by. Now Moses is 80 years old, and it looks like his life has been totally and completely wasted. All the access he had to education, influence, and power has gone down the tubes! His career is at a dead end. He is not the leader of anything. His life is in ruins, he is in the desert surrounded by a bunch of scrawny sheep – that is where we find Moses, and he is 80 years old.

Not only does it look like Moses life has been irreparably ruined, but it looks like the lives God intended Moses to help have been irreparably ruin as well. The Israelites are still under the yoke of oppression. They are still being mistreated with no hope of that ever changing. Then, we get to the end of Exodus chapter 2:23-25.

Guess who God chooses to lead his people out of slavery and oppression. He chooses an 80-year-old broken down, my-career-is-over, my-life-has-been-wasted, former government leader turned shepherd named Moses. Moses not only becomes the leader of a nation at the age of 80. He becomes the role model for what it means to live by faith. It is an unbelievable story of redemption! Most of the things that we read about Moses in the New Testament are of Moses past this experience. We almost pick up with the story when he goes in to set the people of Israel free. But, what, we find here is the backstory of 80 years. What do we learn about this?

First, you can't totally mess up your life, nor can anyone else, if you continue to love God. Actually, I wanted use a stronger word there. When I said "mess up," I wanted to say "screw up," but when I talked with someone about this they said, "You can't say 'screw up' in church," so I said "mess up".

You can't totally mess up your life, and no one can totally mess up your life if you continue to walk with God. On the surface it certainly looked like Moses had completely messed his life up at 80. It certainly appears that the damage he has done to his life is irreparable. But as it turns out, the forty years that Moses spent in the desert were not wasted. It turns out God was at work in the desert, and Moses was open to the work of God in the midst of the desert. The guy who comes out of the desert was a very different guy than the guy that went into the desert. The guy who went into the desert was an arrogant, angry, temper-driven, kind of guy. He comes out a man with all the same skills and abilities, but now that whole package is clothed in humility.

In fact we are told in the Book of Numbers, **"Now, Moses was very humble, more than all men who were on the face of the earth."** [Numbers 12:3 NKJV] Somehow, God took Moses' biggest mistake, the dumbest thing that he had ever done, and wove it into Moses' life in such a way that it made Moses even more usable to God. The Apostle Paul talks about this in Romans 8:28, when he says this**: "And we know that all things work together for good to those who love God, to those who called according to His purpose."** [NKJV] Paul is not saying there that all things are good, because all things are not good. Some things are stupid. Some things are horrible, evil, and exactly opposite from what God desires. All things are not good.

What Paul is saying is that in all things God works for the good in all these things; even the evil things, even the horrible things, even the things that are exactly opposite of what God desires. In all things, God works for the good for those who love Him! For those who continue to love God, no failure is final -- not our own failure, not the failure that someone else has perpetrated upon us. For those who continue to love God, no failure is final. God can weave everything together. He can weave together your obedience and your disobedience. He can weave together your failures and other people's failures. He can take all that and weave it all together into something unbelievably, extraordinarily beautiful.

The second thing that we learn is that it is never, never, never, never, never too late to fulfill God's purpose in your life. It is never too late to have your life, your work, your vocation, or your energy aligned with what God's purpose is for you. Never, never too late! We find in Exodus 2:15 that Moses sat down by a well. Literally, he was sitting between a rock and a hard place. Forty years were ahead. At 40, his life seems over. But, as we find out, at 80 years of age, Moses' life with God is just getting started. This gives me hope folks! The Psalmist David talks about God's ability to help us to discover his purpose for our lives. He describes it this way in Psalm 57:2-3A. **"I will cry out to God most high; To God who performs all things for me. He shall send from heaven and save me."** (NKJV)

The salvation that David is talking about is a salvation that has to do with our eternal destiny. It includes that, but it is more than that. It is about the living out of his redeemed, restored life. It is about the understanding of God's purpose, of our energy, and of our time to be aligned with what God is doing in this world right now. If we cry out to God, if we will return to Him, He will not only forgive the things that need to be forgiven, but He will fulfill His purpose in us!

Some of you are sitting on the rock right now. You are in the midst of your own desert experience and you are wondering if your usefulness to God is over, or at least has been severely limited, maybe by some of the decisions you have made up to this point and maybe by some of the sinful decisions that someone else has made. There is a question of whether your usefulness is too bad and somehow limited.

Maybe you are in the second half of your life and you feel like you have missed your opportunity, wasted your chance, wasted your gifts, or misused your resources up to this point. Maybe you are in the first half of your life and have made some stupid decisions, and you feel you have been placed like on the sidelines for a while. Whatever the circumstances, know that Moses' life teaches us that it is never, never, never, never, never too late to fulfill God's purpose for your life.

There are some of you that are here who need to cry out to God. He needs to save you in the sense that He needs to forgive you. You have made some stupid mistakes and decisions, and you need to confess that. He wants to come alongside of you, and you need to experience His grace to know that your eternal destiny is settled.

As for others of you, that has been settled, but what happens sometimes is that our lives sort of go on autopilot, and we just sort of crank along in the stressful, time-consuming vocations and jobs that we are in. We just miss the purpose for being on this planet. God has a purpose for my life. God has a purpose for your life. It is never too late to cry out to God to ask that His purpose would be fulfilled in the way you live your lives.

It is the alignment issue! It is about how and what am I doing to align with God's purpose for my life. I know that God has a purpose for me. It is never too late. It is never too late to fulfill God's purpose for life. Align things in such a way to fulfill your purpose and God's purpose. Amen!

Appendix Seven

Questions and Answers

This is not a survey, nor is it a thesis. I am answering questions about the gay lifestyle from my own experience. From a mother of a gay son comes this question: "How gay are you? On a continuum from one to a hundred where would you find yourself?" Until I became a Christian, I would say I was forty percent straight and sixty percent gay. For the last sixty years, I have lived a heterosexual or a celibate life without exception. The best answer I can give is that each person must answer that question for himself.

I have a Christian gay friend. That friend said, "Serve God and be celibate." Almost in the same sentence, that friend stated, "Marry yourself to God and the Church." My friend counseled, "Provide places and occasions to have worship and activities such as spiritual retreats. It is not enough to say, "Give your life to God." We must provide places that the individual feels comfortable being themselves in every aspect of their lives. We must pray that they may come to the place where they are able to say, "I am willing to do the one thing that Jesus is asking me to do to become closer to Him and to have fellowship in the Church."

The effects on the family are enormous. It is very traumatic when a family member says for the first time, "I am out of the closet." You are never prepared for it. The family immediately thinks of counseling. The gay person says, "No way," or at least my son did. The family is shocked and does not have any idea how to act. The gay person has made a statement, and the statement appears to cry out for acceptance. The family needs to make a definite commitment to their son or daughter that they still love them without reserve. The alternative is that they will go to where they are accepted without reserve. They will experience aloneness in spite of the fact that they may have many friends. The family, on the other hand, will cry tears of anguish for a child that has left the nest and whom they cannot reach. The individual and the family must keep all their options open. Keep them open!

A young person that I was recently talking with asked this question, "How do you approach being gay when no one seems to wants to talk about it?" My answer is to be a friend. Be yourself. Do not compromise your faith in God's word or what you believe. The person that you are trying to reach must know that you live what you believe. Jesus was faithful with the woman at the well in Samaria. Because of Jesus' relationship with this one woman, the apostles were able to experience revival in the early church. His compassion did not stop him from saying to the woman taken in adultery, "Has any one condemned you?" She replied, "No." His answer was, "Neither do I condemn you, go and sin no more." We must be as accepting as Jesus was. If we are to reach our world for Christ, we need be true to what we believe.

Pornography is taboo for any relationship. It is cheating on one another, no matter what the orientation, and it is not honoring to God. On the other hand, if the person is celebrating recovery, they will find it all the harder to live the way they want to live.

In every phase of my Christian Life and ministry, I have had accountability partners. I have had men that I could trust to have my back. They knew the battle I was fighting, and they watched that I might be true to my faith. I have always wanted to walk in integrity and faithfulness in my Christian life. There have been times that they have advised me, "Be careful," and they meant it for my benefit. Thank God for those who have watched out for my back!

This may not answer all of your questions. However, in a culture and society with different lifestyles, it should provide food for thought. It should provide answers to some questions that are left unanswered.

Please remember to find a trusted friend to help you think through your questions. My bibliography has been provided for anyone interested in doing research in order that they may have good answers to their questions. The best answer is you, and how your needs might be met. Trust not only your research, but also trust the Bible to lead you to where you desire to be, no matter your lifestyle.

Appendix Eight

Plans of Salvation (NKJV)

My plan is to give you some Biblical tools to enable you to lead an individual to a saving knowledge of Christ. First, I will give you four Bible lessons that will facilitate leading someone to Christ. Secondly, I want to give you the Roman Road to Salvation. Thirdly, I want to give you a simple question to ask that seems to facilitate a positive response at any time, and lastly I want to give you a simple prayer that will be helpful in allowing people to make a commitment to Jesus Christ as Savior and Lord.

Psalm 24:1-10 [Read]

First, I like to read the entire Psalm through. This allows the person you are trying to lead to Christ to be a little bit familiar with the Psalm. Secondly, verse three asks us a question that each of us have asked in our own way, **"Who may ascend the hill of the Lord? Or who may stand in His holy place?"** Verse four gives us the answer. He who has clean hands (His sins forgiven), and a pure heart (made pure by the Word of God through the Holy Spirit). The last half of verse four gives some conditions, **"Who has not lifted up his soul to an idol?"** (In other words, Jesus is number one). **"Nor sworn deceitfully."** (You are not just saying it, but you mean it). Friend, is there any reason that you cannot receive Jesus right now? Be prepared to lead them in the prayer of commitment.

John 3:1-8 [Read]

You must always know what you are talking about. Read carefully John 3:1-21, and be able to explain the story in your own words. You will note that Jesus makes three profound statements to **Nicodemus "Most assuredly, I say to you, unless one is born again, he cannot see the kingdom of God."** After Nicodemus's question in verse four, Jesus answered, **"Most assuredly, I say to you, unless a man is born of the water and the Spirit, he cannot enter the kingdom of God."** Jesus reaffirmed this by saying to Nicodemus the third time, **"Do not marvel that I said to you, 'You must be born again.'"** You may want to highlight verse eight, and certainly verse sixteen, the golden verse of the Bible. Here again, you may ask, "Friend, is there any reason that you cannot receive Jesus right now?" Be prepared to lead them in the prayer of commitment.

Ephesians 2:1-10 [Read]

This passage is good for an affirmation of faith or leading a person to a personal commitment. I have used this for both, and I have used it often just to remember what God has done for me or the other person. One thought is appropriate, "Be prepared." The Apostle Paul reminds them of three things. First, he tells them who they were. Secondly, he reminds them of what God had done for them. Finally, he explained how God worked in their life. It goes without saying that he wants to work in each individual life in the same manner. Be sure to read verses 8-10 in sequence. Paul is very careful to point out that we do not work our way into Heaven. We work after our way into Heaven is assured. Here again is that question, "Friend is there any reason that you cannot receive Jesus right now as your Savior and Lord?" Be prepared to lead them in the prayer of commitment.

1 John 1:1-10 [Read]

This is my favorite. I especially like this chapter when leading a young person to the Lord. Picture if you will, the apostle John at about 92 years of age, with a long flowing beard. Look at Jesus through John's eyes. This Godly old man tells us why he is writing, in order that we might have fellowship with us, and with the Father and His Son Jesus, and then he concludes with, **"And these things we write unto you that your joy may be full."** Read the rest of the verses with expression, and as you have experienced it. After this reading, you may go back to verse nine. Be prepared to ask them if there is any reason they cannot accept Jesus as they pray with you verse nine in their own words. You may use the prayer of commitment as you feel appropriate.

The Roman Road:

This is great for an older person especially. However, it may be used at any age level. You must be prepared if you use this plan of salvation. Be sure to have Paul's Epistle to the Romans well read and your Bible handy. Mark your Bible so that each verse may be easy to turn to in your Bible.

The Gospel – The just shall live by faith. (1:16-17)

All have sinned – the Gentile, the Hebrew, all mankind have sinned. (3:10, 12, 20, 23)

"God demonstrates His own love toward us – in that while we were sinners Christ died for us." (5:8, ref. 5:12)

"The gift of God is eternal life" (6:23) – "Whoever shall call on the Lord Jesus Christ shall be saved." (10:10)

Receive and Act – "Confess with your mouth - Believe in your heart." (Vv.9-10; Ref. 3:20)

The Apostle asks us to make a Spiritual Sacrifice. (12:1-2)

You may now ask your question, "Friend is there any reason that you cannot receive Jesus as your Savior right now?" You may use the prayer of commitment as you feel would be appropriate in each individual occasion.

Prayer of Commitment:

Dear Lord Jesus, I recognize my need of you. I confess my sin and/or my need of you, and I ask you to come into my heart and life. I want to accept you as my Savior and to serve you as my Lord. I ask you to lead me in every area of my life. In your name I pray. Amen!

There are two things I leave with you. Be prepared, and always close the occasion with your prayer for that particular person, no matter what his/her decision may have been. God bless you as you serve Our Wonderful Savior.

Manual One

The Church Reaches Out

"How does the Church Reach Out to the Gay Community?"

"Rejoice Evermore. Pray without ceasing. In everything give thanks, for this is the will of God in Christ Jesus concerning you. Do not quench the Spirit." (1 Thessalonians 5:13-19 NKJV)

This is a question that two pastors asked me recently. I have mulled over my answer for about a month. I have talked to several people about their thoughts. One person gave me three points to consider. 1) Accept them. 2) Love them. 3) Do not be homophobic. That was good advice and I appreciated the advice.

God gave me this advice. First, I needed to pray. I needed to pray for myself. What is going to be my role in reaching out to that or any community? If I am in a leadership role, I need to pray that God will bring others alongside me. I need someone that will have my back. I need to have prayer partners, both within my family and my church. I need to pray that God will direct me in how to have the local church gain awareness about the ministry and that the church will begin praying for the ministry. This ministry must be saturated with prayer at every stage as the local church reaches out to the gay community. I believe that as they begin to pray for the gay community, they will come to own the ministry as well.

There are two other words that need to be considered. The first of the two is "acceptance." You will need to accept them as they are. The church body will have to be a real part of accepting those we are trying to reach out to with spiritual values. They have stepped out of the closet. Therefore, we need to provide an atmosphere that they can accept. Our goal needs to be one that they eventually will embrace and will be able to walk with God in integrity even as they fight the battle of living for Jesus.

The second word that we need to consider is protection. We need to protect them. The church is not always kind. We need to protect the congregation. This will entail having the congregation know and be able to come alongside the individual. Also, because of the general church policy, we need to provide a secure environment for our children through adulthood. This brings us to an additional word, "security."

The individual must be secure both in the church and in the community of which they are currently a part. This will necessitate having a group of people that can be trusted to be quiet and be able to observe the HIPPA laws that are in effect when you reach out to people who need medical support. It may necessitate availability of counseling on a professional level. It will necessitate having the gay community accepts the security that must be in place because of our culture. Our goal is the eternal salvation of the individual. Everyone involved has to know that there are boundaries.

Our Heavenly Father, please help us as we reach out to those that need You! Help us to reach out in prayer, acceptance, protection, and security for everyone that is involved. Lord Jesus, we ask You to bless us as we reach out to those that need to know You as their personal Savior in spite of their lifestyle. Amen!

Manual Two

Rehabilitation and Transformation

This model was originally for my home Church and community. I have edited and tried to modify it in a generic sense to make it usable by any church or locale. (This model is especially appropriate for the Sexual Offender)

Denominational Oversight:

To be endorsed by the General Church Endorsing Agent for a LBGT ministry

To have an interview with the Conference of Association Leader

To obtain the Local Pastor's support and direction

To secure the permission of the Local Church Board of Administration for permission to form a ministry to the Lesbian, Gay, Bisexual and Transgendered Community (LGBT)

Community Advisory Group: (Five Members)

The Sheriff

The local Mayor

The local Chief of Police

Health Department (Mental) Designee

Area Churches & Clergy

This group is advisory. It **is meant to be supportive, especially when working with sexual offenders.** You cannot go it alone. They will meet once a year. The Board of Directors may submit their Annual Report to them. They may be contacted by the R&T Board of Directors officers in an advisory capacity as needed.

Board of Directors for Local Church: (Minimum of Seven Members)

Officers

Chairperson

Vice-Chairperson

Secretary

Treasurer

Chaplain or Lead Person for ministry to the Gay Community: Executive Director for one three-year term.

Their purpose is to expedite, to advocate, and to provide spiritual service to the gay community and to sexual offenders in the local community and to provide a means of re-entry to the local Church and into community in a meaningful relationship.

Things to do:

Touch base with the Endorsing Agent.

Meet with the members listed in the "Community Advisory Group".

Meet with the Leadership Team (Board of Administration) of the Local Church.

Establish guidelines for use of Church facilities.

Guidelines:

Maintain confidentiality in/out of the Group. **This is a must.** "What is said here stays here."

Identify with a local Church.

You must be aware of the guidelines/rules of the local Church. (What you can and cannot do).

Interview with the Lead Pastor of the church or his/her designee.

The local Church needs to establish an in-house "security system" that will protect all segments of the church congregation.

What is the Answer?

What is a desirable message to communicate to this support group? I do not have an answer. The answer lies within the individuals and their relationship with God. Do I obey God's mandate or not? If I am to be obedient to the Word of God, what must I do to enrich my life and to receive the help I need to be able to live a productive life within the local community?

Manual Three

Pastoral Guidelines

After writing "The Church Reaches Out" and "Rehabilitation and Transformation," I felt it was wise to get the advice of my Lead Pastor. There needs to be guidelines that we are all aware of to keep us on the same page. These guidelines are here to keep that communication in proper perspective. This does not supersede normal pastoral relationships with people to whom we are ministering. It is fully based in Biblical truth.

1. That the Lead Pastor or his/her designee will interview each prospective member of a group to advise them concerning the guidelines for the individual and the church's needs concerning prayer, acceptance, protection and security for all concerned.

2. That a group will meet for a designated time period of eight to ten weeks with at least a month break in between the start of a new group.

3. That in a men's, group that there will be two men leading at all times. Or, in the case of a mixed group there will be two women and two men leading the group. There may be husband and wife teams in mixed groups.

4. That a report of the group accomplishments will be made to the Lead Pastor and the Board of Administration and/or Pastor's Cabinet at the end of each session. This will not include personal and confidential information.

Number four above will entail the setting and accomplishing of goals for the group. For instance how many in the group? What format will the meetings have?

Recommended Readings

I am providing recommended readings for the express purpose of helping you to find pertinent information. I have included books that have helped me on my journey. I do want to highlight several of them here. This will help anyone desiring to read and/or to do research.

First, un-christian by David Kinnaman is listed as it gives the way to the young gay community looks at the church and the believer, as researched by the Barna Group. You will not want to miss chapter five. They say we are bigoted, homophobic hypocrites.

Second, I highly recommend Love is an Orientation, by Andrew Marin. It is about how the believer and the church should look at the LGBT Community.

Third, Reclaiming Surrendered Ground by Jim Logan and Competent to Counsel by Jay E. Adams are good books that may help you to claim surrendered ground and to counsel respectively. The two books will help the individual as well as anyone leading a group or individual counseling to counsel wisely.

Fourth, I have found the book by Henri J.M. Nouwen, Sabbatical Journey, very helpful in coming to understand myself.

Fifth, I want to list Homosexuality and the Christian, by Mark A. Yarhouse, PsyD. He writes about sexual orientation, same-sex attraction, and sexual identity as they pertain to the Christian that is plagued with homosexual issues.

Lastly, my paper, "The Problems of the Homosexual In and Out of the Criminal Justice System" in the AEIC Journal, January 1979, may help you to see another side of the equation.

SELECTED REFERENCES (BIBLIOGRAPHY)

H. O. Wiley, Introduction to Christian Theology; Beacon Hill Press, Kansas City, MO (6th Printing 1954).

Random House Webster's, College Dictionary, Random House, New York, 2000.

David Kinnaman and Gabe Lyons, un Christian, Baker House, Grand Rapids, MI 2007.

Andrew Marin, Love is an Orientation, "Elevation the conversation with the Gay Community", IVP Books, Downers Grove, Illinois. 2009.

Mark A. Yarhouse, PsyD. Homosexuality and the Christian, Bethany House Publishers, Minneapolis, Minnesota, 2010.

Jim Logan, Reclaiming Surrendered Ground, Moody Press, Chicago, Illinois, 1995.

Jay E. Adams, Competent to Counsel; ISBN 9780310511403, Presbyterian Press, Nuttley, NJ.

Stephen Arterburn, Fred Stoeker with Mike Yorkey, every young man's battle; Waterbrook Press, Colorado Springs, Co 2002.

Shannon Ethridge and Stephen Arterburn with Josh McDowell, every young woman's battle; Waterbrook Press, Colorado Springs, Co 2004.

Henri J. M. Nouwen, Sabbatical Journey: "The diary of his final year"; The Crosswind Publishing Company, New York, 1998.

2011 Book of Discipline, "The Free Methodist Church – USA"; Light and Life Communications, Indianapolis, ID, 2012.

Lane A. Scott and Leon O. Hynson, Editors, <u>Christian Ethics</u>, "Wesleyan Theological Perspectives"; Warner Press, Inc. 1983.

Association Evangelical Institutional Chaplains, <u>Journal, July 1979, No. 7</u>; "The Problem of the Homosexuality In and Out of the Criminal Justice System" William T. Lowery, Sr. page 33, Arlington, VA.

Tom Fette, Ed. <u>The Celebration Hymnal</u>, "Songs and Hymns for Worship"; Word Music/Integrity Music, USA 1997.

EPILOGUE

The Bush Still Burns. I was born along the south side of Sandy Creek, in Western Pennsylvania. I was raised and tutored in Jefferson and McKean Counties. They were great times. I entered the United States Navy and had my final discharge in December, 1952, after about two and a half months in jail. I spent about twelve years on the backside of my Median Desert before I was in regular Christian ministry in 1964. They were great years of learning and serving Him. Beginning in November 1974, I served 33 years by going to jail as a chaplain and 27 years in camping ministries. Finally, the Triune God got my attention. He called me to serve the lesbian, gay, bisexual and transgendered community (LGBT). After about 25 years, I answered with a weak "Yes." God brought me to the place where I could see the burning bush that was not consumed. There was that time of a wilderness trek. I have rounded the tip of my Dead Sea. There will be times of going through the wilderness similar to Edom, Moab, and Ammon. The Israelites will be represented by the people that I reach out to with the Love of God. They will be gathered, figuratively, on the Plains of Gilead opposite Jericho. One day, God will ask me to climb my Mount Nebo, to view my promised land. There will be no end. I will not see the Holy Land of Palestine. I will see a Gate of Pearl. I will hear, "Take off your shoes". I will do so and walk through the Gate of Pearl with bare feet of service for the ground on which I will stand will be Holy ground for all eternity. One day I too will return with Moses and Elijah, along with all God's people of all time when the Lord Jesus comes for the second time to claim His own at the bodily resurrection of the dead. Amen!